More Scrambles
in the
Canadian Rockies

Andrew Nugara

VANCOUVER • VICTORIA • CALGARY

Rocky Mountain Books
#108 – 17665 66A Avenue
Surrey, BC V3S 2A7
www.rmbooks.com

Rocky Mountain Books
PO Box 468
Custer, WA
98240-0468

Library and Archives Canada Cataloguing in Publication

Nugara, Andrew
    More scrambles in the Canadian Rockies / Andrew Nugara.

Includes bibliographical references.
ISBN 978-1-894765-86-2

1. Rocky Mountains, Canadian (B.C. and Alta.)—Guidebooks. 2. Free climbing—
Rocky Mountains, Canadian (B.C. and Alta.)—Guidebooks. 3. Hiking—Rocky
Mountains, Canadian (B.C. and Alta.)—Guidebooks. I. Title.

FC219.N94 2007   796.522'09711   C2006-906767-8

Library of Congress Control Number: 2006940298

Edited by Matt Jennings
Book design by John Luckhurst
Cover design by John Luckhurst
All cover and interior photographs provided by Andrew and Mark Nugara
unless otherwise noted.

Printed in Canada

Rocky Mountain Books acknowledges the financial support for its publishing
program from the Government of Canada through the Book Publishing Industry
Development Program (BPIDP), Canada Council for the Arts, and the province
of British Columbia through the British Columbia Arts Council and the Book
Publishing Tax Credit.

Contents

Near the summit of Old Goat Mountain, looking south.

On the ridge between Lorette (behind) and "Skogan Peak."

On Vimy Peak, overlooking Middle Waterton Lake and Mount Crandell.

At the col between Kent Ridge-North and GR244254.

Looking east along the ridge of Mount Bryant.

Jodi Soare and the author leave the summit of Mount Glendowan.

Taking in beautiful scenery from the summit of "Kananaskis Peak."

Early season snow hits the ridge of Mount James Walker.

James Wright tackles a more challenging route on Wind Mountain.

The summit block of "Piggy Plus". Mount Sir Douglas to the right.

A late-season ascent of the east ridge of Mount Head.

Linda Breton on the connecting ridge between St. Eloi and Syncline.

Looking toward Mount Loomis, from the Odlum/Loomis col.

A rare scene of low-lying cloud blanketing the valley, as seen from the Loomis/Odlum col.

Preface

Thanks in large part to Alan Kane and his outstanding guidebook, *Scrambles in the Canadian Rockies*, my life changed in a way that I least expected in July of 2001. My brother, Mark, dragged me up Grizzly Peak via the route described in Kane's book. Though the experience initially left me wanting nothing more than to sit at home with a good book instead of repeating the ordeal, I did return to try another scramble, and another, and in short order Mark and I were both completely hooked. From then on, a trip to the beautiful mountains of the Canadian Rockies became a weekly ritual. We later took an avalanche safety course, a snow-and-ice weekend, and an introductory rock climbing course to better prepare ourselves for more challenging objectives. Through it all, however, scrambling, or unroped climbing, remained the primary focus of our trips.

At the same time that we had completed approximately half of the scrambles in Kane's book, we started to become more and more interested in ascending mountains not in the book, often for which there were no route descriptions available. We found the experiences to be challenging and enormously gratifying, especially if we were able to make it to the top. In time, we had built up a small collection of ascents, and Mark suggested that I compile the information into a sequel to Kane's book. Once started, the book pretty much wrote itself—after all, the mountains are always there, we simply had to find an interesting route up each one. I was also lucky enough to receive invaluable route information and advice from other scramblers, which made the task of ascending each mountain that much easier.

If new to the hobby of scrambling, I strongly recommend that you pick up a copy of Alan Kane's *Scrambles in the Canadian Rockies* and complete a number of the easy and moderate ascents described in that book before tackling trips in this book. This is not at all to suggest that the ascents in this volume are of greater difficulty than the scrambles in Kane's book. In fact, I would say that, in general, the scrambling is easier in this volume. However, as another generalization, I would say that the ascents in this book involve longer approaches and perhaps require a little more physical stamina. In addition, many of these scrambles take you far from the road and have a remote feel to them. More than likely, you or your party will be alone throughout the ascent, with help a long way off. Kane's book is also full of useful and interesting information not repeated in this volume.

Acknowledgements

Of course, I am indebted to Alan Kane, whose guidebook, *Scrambles in the Canadian Rockies*, provided the primary inspiration for this sequel edition. Kane's book is the scrambler's Bible, and everyone who aspires to ascend peaks of the Canadian Rockies should have a copy. As well, thanks must be given to Alan Kane, who has graciously allowed us to reprint his Introduction from *Scrambles in the Canadian Rockies*, in this volume (page 3 to 13). Alan's information will always be an invaluable asset to scrambles.

Gillean Daffern's two-volume set, *Kananaskis Country Trail Guide*, is another extremely well-written and invaluable resource. The ragged edges of both volumes in my possession attest to how much I have used them over the years.

My sincerest thanks to the following people for ideas, route information, support, and encouragement: Dave Stephens, Sonny Bou, Bob Spirko, Dinah Kruze, Linda Breton, Kevin Barton, Bob Parr, Kyle Oak, Vern Dewit, Bill Kerr, Gillean and Tony Daffern, Bennet Wong, Frank Nelson, Rafal Kazmierczak, Stuart Brideaux, and Mitch Brown.

A special thanks to Julie Baker for proof-reading and correcting the plethora of mistakes in the original manuscript, and also to all the folks at Rocky Mountain Books, who have all been nothing but delightful to work with.

Our mum has always been a tremendous support for Mark and me. On our weekly Sunday visit, she has listened to more than one tale describing an epic day (or two) in the mountains. Mum always manages a non-judgmental, "Just be careful out there, boys." Thanks Mum.

Most of all, this guidebook would not have been possible were it not for my brother, Mark, who introduced me to scrambling, encouraged me to author this book, and accompanied me on the majority of the ascents. As well as a terrific scrambling partner, Mark has been an incredible source of inspiration to me. Not for a single second has Mark allowed his condition—he is legally blind—to deter him from his enjoyment of the mountains. This book is as much his accomplishment as it is mine. Thanks Bro!

Introduction

Scrambling is getting to the top of a mountain without technical gear (i.e. ropes, climbing protection, etc.) or technical climbing techniques, though the occasional use of climbing techniques may be required for particularly difficult sections or moves. In the strictest sense of the term, scrambling involves the use of the hands to ascend or descend terrain. That is what distinguishes it from steep hiking. However, anyone who has completed a number of scrambles in the Canadian Rockies knows full well that the overwhelming majority of scrambles involve a significant amount of hiking and many never require use of the hands. Thus, some of the scrambles that earn an "easy" rating could probably be more accurately described as steep hikes. Regardless of the terminology you use, scrambling can be one of the most rewarding ways to enjoy the beauty of the natural world that surrounds us, and you get a physical workout that is second to none at the same time.

Scrambling has a few advantages over other forms of mountain recreation. Since scrambling is non-technical and doesn't require the use of a rope, scramblers can move at a very fast rate, covering considerable horizontal and vertical distances in a short amount of time. A quick perusal of the estimated round-trip times of the scrambles in this book will immediately reveal why this is important.

Though all human activity in the mountains has negative impacts on the environment and wildlife, scramblers and hikers can keep those impacts to a bare minimum. More so than most other groups of mountain users, scramblers leave the environment in exactly the way they found it—no pitons, bolts, tattered webbing and slings, rappel stations, and other climbing paraphernalia are left behind. No one will ever clear-cut a large section of land for scramblers, as the ski resorts see fit to do for skiers. On the downside, the above mentioned ability for scramblers to move fast enables them to venture into remote areas that would otherwise be spared the detriments of human intrusion. This means that scramblers and hikers simply have to be extremely cognizant of their responsibilities and obligations to leave these remote areas in the same state they were found in and have as little impact as possible while they are there.

There is no question that nine times out of ten the best view is from the top. The visual rewards of making it to the top of a mountain are often unequalled. There are few things better in life than the unobstructed view of the surrounding area from a mountaintop on a cloudless day, be it summer, spring, autumn, or winter. More than likely, you will also encounter innumerable wondrous scenes and views on the way up. And every mountain is a completely unique experience, even when two trips are within very close proximity of each other.

As well, the emotional and mental rewards of scrambling can be an end unto themselves, and I don't think saying that scrambling can be addictive is a misrepresentation of the word. I'm sure that every scrambler can re-live, in vivid detail, the elation of taking the final steps few steps to the summit of a particularly challenging or interesting mountain.

Back to reality for the final word! It cannot be stressed enough that scrambling can be extremely dangerous. If you have not done so already, please read the sections "Gradings" and "Avoiding Death by Scrambling," written by Alan Kane and found on pages 5 and 12 respectively, as well as the section "Scrambling vs. Climbing" on page 19. It could save your life. In addition, Tom Morin's recent book *A Hiker's Guide to Scrambling Safety*, is an excellent reference for all hikers and scramblers. The book offers detailed and invaluable information to help make your scrambling experience as safe as possible.

Enjoy the mountains, appreciate them, cherish them, be thankful for the great privilege we are afforded in having access to them, and above all, take care of them. How we treat the environment defines us as a species as much as how we treat each other. Throughout history we have failed consistently on the latter and the last one hundred years or so have proven us to be equally inept on the former—let's ensure we all improve on both counts.

Looking northeast from the summit of Victoria Peak in the Castle.

Scrambling in the Canadian Rockies

BY ALAN KANE

The Canadian Rockies are truly one of the great mountains ranges of the world and are unique in many ways. Although they do not attain the lofty 14,000-ft. elevations of their counterparts in the United States, the Canadian Rockies are undeniably craggier and more impressive. Similarly, while particular peaks in the Cascade Range of the Pacific North West may be somewhat more rugged, many barely rise above the tree line. The volcanoes, obviously, are an exception. Yet upon reaching the summit of a Cascade volcano, one sees perhaps only two or three other volcanoes rising skyward with few summits of note in between.

Europe's Alps may outshine Canada's Rockies for sheer magnificence of form, but sadly from every summit one sees a proliferation of mountain railways, gondola lifts, roads, and hotels. The climber pampers himself in warm huts offering hot meals, wine, and bedding. Route-finding involves following paint splotches and hordes of other people, and, not surprisingly, the feeling of wilderness has long since disappeared.

Great ranges like the Himalayas and the Andes do surpass the Rockies in many respects, but access can be both dangerous and difficult. To many, simply staying healthy throughout the visit presents a considerable challenge, never mind trying to reach a summit.

By comparison, Canada's Rockies boast the grandeur of innumerable craggy, glaciated peaks, difficult and remote, yet also offer myriad easier ascents close to roads. Glacially scoured basins contain pristine alpine lakes and flower-strewn meadows. Elk, bear, and moose roam free, and from every mountaintop one witnesses an endless sea of summits—entertainment for a lifetime. Welcome to the Canadian Rockies!

Climate and Season

Summer in the Canadian Rockies is short. Sometimes it doesn't even show up. The climbing season is highly affected by weather patterns, and conditions in any given area vary from year to year and range to range. An old-timer once remarked that a year in the Rockies is ten months of winter and two months of poor sleddin'. He probably hadn't visited the Columbia Icefields: twelve months of good sleddin'!

The early scrambling season is confined to the eastern part of the Rockies in the front ranges. These areas are generally a little warmer and experience less precipitation, whether snow or rain. Typical examples of these areas lie east of Canmore, east of Jasper and in parts of the Crowsnest Pass. Here, south and west-facing slopes come into condition as early as May and June. East-facing slopes require a few weeks more. North-facing slopes take longer yet, and in a cold, wet year, snow patches persist all year.

Travelling farther west in the Rockies, temperatures are slightly cooler and precipitation is greater, especially along the Continental Divide and the Main Ranges. Lake Louise is wetter then Banff, which is wetter than the Kananaskis Valley. Some of the most inclement weather occurs at the Columbia Icefields between Lake Louise and Jasper. The mean yearly temperature is a brisk –2.1° C, making Banff's + 2.5° balmy by comparison. Farther south, Denver, Colorado tops in at a sizzling +10°! Tropical, you might say.

Not only are the Main Ranges cooler, but they also include the highest peaks. It is often mid-July or later before snow-free climbing conditions occur here. Ideal conditions may be as brief as a couple of weeks or may not even occur in a cool, wet year. Conversely, an extended autumn or Indian Summer can stretch the scrambling season past September, up to October and even into November. In 1997, a powerful El Niño year, folks were still bagging peaks in early December. Autumn often rewards the optimist with crisp mornings, periods of stable weather, and no crowds or insects. The drawback is the shorter daylight.

Registration

Voluntary registration is available in provincial and national parks at warden and ranger offices and at the information centre in Kananaskis Country. Registration gives park staff justification for purchasing rescue equipment and maintaining trained personnel, so it is a worthwhile step based on that alone. Remember, if you do register, you are legally required to sign in upon returning. If you fail to sign in, an unnecessary and costly search could be initiated, and YOU can be billed for the entire amount. BE AWARE THAT RESCUES ARE NEVER INITIATED UNTIL THE FOLLOWING DAY, so you should always carry warm clothing, extra clothing, and be prepared to survive a night out. It is worthwhile informing others of your plans, or, if you do not register, leave an itinerary somewhere in your vehicle. Eventually authorities will scour it for clues and will know where to pick up your body to keep the mountains pristine. At the time of writing, the cost of rescues is still borne by the Canadian taxpayer, but with government budget cutbacks this may well change in the future. Although the rescue budget in one park in a recent year amounted to much less than 0.5 percent of their total budget, outdoor adventures in the mountains are perceived by government as generating little direct revenue, and by some taxpayers as being a drain on finances. This misinformation makes us an easy target. Accordingly, future rescue budgets may be reduced with the shortfall being covered through some form of a surcharge. This is in spite of a hefty price increase in park passes coupled with the imposition of backcountry overnight fees.

Permits

All visitors stopping in a national park require a valid national park pass, available at park entrance gates and information centres. In addition, overnight stays in the national park backcountry campsites require a backcountry permit and cost about $8 per night. Reservations may also be required in certain heavily used areas, such as Skoki near Lake Louise. At the time of writing, there are no additional permits required for picnicking, sightseeing, photographing, or shopping—yet!

Times and Directions

In this book, suggested round-trip time covers a range and is based both on personal experience and that of acquaintances. This time assumes the participant is fit, able, and doesn't dawdle. Persons who hike, bike, and jog regularly should fall into this category. Anyone who occasionally strolls the interpretive paths for exercise will be out of their league on these scrambles. A general guideline for a comfortable ascent pace is 300 m (1,000 ft.) per hour, and fit parties will have few problems maintaining this pace.

Directions given are referenced relative to the direction of travel and where any doubt might arise, a compass bearing is included, too.

Gradings

First of all, ratings only apply when conditions are DRY. Simple descriptions of easy, moderate, and difficult have been adopted, and, where appropriate, additional information, such as exposure (potential fall distance), may be included. This grading system does not equate directly to existing systems of grading climbs. Easy and moderate scrambles are in the UIAA class I to class II range. Scrambles rated as difficult would normally be about YDS class 3 to 4, UIAA class –III. In some instances there could be a move or two approaching fifth class. For example, Old Goat Mountain may have a section of about 5.2 or 5.3, but the routes do not generally involve any climbing near that level. A better explanation of these ratings might be:

Easy—mostly hiking, much hands in pockets stuff, little exposure, no maintained trails. Not surprisingly, most easy scrambles are not scrambles at all but are mostly off-trail hiking. Lost Mountain and Vimy Ridge are prime examples. UIAA Class I.

Moderate—frequent use of handholds required, possible exposure but not usually enough to be a "death fall." Some route-finding involved. e.g. Drywood Mountain and Victoria Peak. UIAA Class II.

Difficult—much use of handholds required, sections may be steep, loose, and exposed, or rock could be smooth and downsloping. Fall distance may be significant enough to be fatal. Route-finding skills are generally necessary to determine the most practical and feasible way for specific sections. Less experienced parties might prefer the security of a climbing rope for short sections, and being off-route may well require technical climbing. Anyone with vertigo or a fear of heights should avoid scrambles rated as difficult. (Sounds logical, but you'd be surprised.) Examples are Old Goat Mountain, Mount Dungarvan, and the west ridge of Mount Baldy's West Peak. YDS 3rd or 4th Class, rarely YDS Class 5 or UIAA Class III.

As compared to other forms of rock such as quartzite, limestone is a high-friction medium. Nonetheless, when wet, snowy, or icy, scramble routes become much harder. Many scrambles are then climbs and mountaineering ascents that require technical climbing gear and the use of anchors and belay techniques. THESE SCRAMBLE RATINGS ARE APPLICABLE ONLY IN OPTIMAL CONDITIONS: DRY AND FREE OF SNOW. Some years dry conditions may not even occur on some routes.

Equipment

The best footwear for scrambling is a pair of sturdy leather boots with a cleated Vibram sole and a half or three-quarter shank for rigidity. Running shoes and ultra-light hiking boots are unsuitable, giving too little ankle support and protection on talus slopes. They also wear out quickly. At the other extreme are plastic mountaineering boots with an insulated liner. These are hot, sweaty, and clumsy. Save those dainty dancing slippers for ice routes and glaciers.

Ski or hiking poles are steadily gaining favour in North America and the Rockies and are a great asset on scree slopes. They especially save wear and tear on the knees on descent and are invaluable for stream crossings. The three-section collapsible models are easily stowed in a pack and weigh little. Careful—they can collapse unexpectedly! Recommended.

Clothing

Versatility is the key word in dressing for success in the mountains. Functional synthetics that can be layered to protect against a wide variety of mountain weather and temperatures are what the fashionable scramblers are wearing this season. This wardrobe should include a raincoat (made of material such as GoreTex), windpants, toque, wool gloves, cap, pile or fleece jacket, a wool or synthetic shirt, and a synthetic undershirt. A pair of calf-height gaiters keeps debris out of boots. Although cotton shirts depicting bears and loons may be fine on Main Street Banff, they provide little warmth when wet and are downright miserable on a chilly mountaintop. Damp clothing can result in a drop in body core temperature, a condition known as hypothermia. Further deterioration can result in death. This condition includes cold hands and feet, fatigue, irritability, excessive shivering, dullness, inability to use hands, lack of coordination, slurred speech, apathy, and irrational actions. And all because of a loon shirt! But seriously, should any of these symptoms be present, get the victim into the warmest, driest clothing available. Have him eat and drink (not alcohol), and get him moving toward tree line and home. If he cannot continue, build a fire to warm him up. When you do get him back to safety, buy him a warmer shirt. Hypothermia is easier to prevent than it is to treat.

Necessary Extras

Good sunblock cream (spf 15 or more), glacier glasses or good sunglasses that eliminate UV rays, lip sunscreen, compass, 1-litre water bottle, a large handkerchief, and toilet paper identify the "old hand" versus the newcomer on the mountain. Consider carrying a small first aid kit, either homemade or commercially packed. No trip is complete without pictures, and what better excuse for a break than to take a photo or two?

Hazards

BY ALAN KANE

Mountains are inherently dangerous places. Scrambling is a dangerous undertaking in an inherently dangerous place. Increased demand for adventure is revealing a disturbing trend in the populace. It is an attitude problem, and it is people's penchant for passing the blame when they get in trouble. Sure, this adventure stuff makes great conversation, but when an accident happens, blame yourself and no one else. If you cannot take responsibility for your actions, do the rest of us a favour and stay home. Unlike the United States, where individuals have successfully won large sums of money in ridiculous negligence lawsuits, precedent-setting cases in Canada have taken a much more sensible approach. The onus of responsibility has been placed squarely on the participant—right where it belongs. How refreshing! Forewarned is forearmed, though, so here are some hazards that can occur in the mountains.

Rockfall

It should come as no surprise that the Canadian Rockies habour more than their share of loose rock. Witness the huge slopes of rubble that provide easy routes to the top. The Canadian Rockies are composed primarily of limestone, with lesser amounts of quartzite in areas near the Continental Divide. The overall quality of the rock is often poor and handholds may pull out unexpectedly. A good thump with your hand will often give a hint of how solid the hold is. "Good rock" is a relative term and it may lie under much loose rubble, especially on ledges. Anyone with an aversion to loose rock and rubble will find few scrambles in the Canadian Rockies to their liking. Besides the danger of loose handholds, another, perhaps greater threat is party-induced rockfall.

Rockfall can kill. Apparently, some parties are oblivious to the dangers of flying rock. Often, with a bit of thought and care, one can ascend even loose, steep terrain and knock down virtually nothing. Unthinking or bumbling individuals, on the other hand, may unleash virtual torrents of stones. These become deadly missiles to anyone below, even when wearing a helmet. Have you ever had the terrifying experience of hearing a rock suddenly whiz by close to your head, or having it bound down the slope in your direction? If so, then you should have a good idea of the consequences of being hit: major facial injuries, a broken arm, a concussion, or death. Though it is not recommended you climb below others, if you are the upper party, taking this as license to be careless is both ignorant and dangerous. Remember that a helmet protects only the head. While many scramble routes are not steep enough for this hazard to be of concern, be wary of steeper routes, particularly gullies. Gullies act as funnels for dislodged debris, and in these you should be particularly careful.

Weather

Fickle is probably the best description for mountain weather. Rain, snow, and thunderstorms can and do occur with almost no warning throughout much of the scrambling season. All may occur during a single afternoon. You might even get sunshine, too. Temperatures can dip below freezing in the Rockies even in the middle of summer, while temperatures on a hot scree slope may cause heatstroke. Weather forecasts sound downright convincing when they predict those warm, sunny weekends, but be forewarned: Conditions can change rapidly. Mountain weather forecasting in the Canadian Rockies is far from an exact science. Many a climbing group have been caught off guard on a big peak when severe weather arrived unexpectedly. Epics and deaths have occurred as a result. Keep your eyes open for changes. Of interest are the new digital watches with altimeters and built-in barometric trend indicators. If you've invested in one of these, a decline in air pressure overnight may warn of deteriorating weather over the next twenty-four hours.

Avalanches

On most open south and west-facing ridge routes, snowslides occur early in the season and do not pose a serious avalanche threat to scramblers except in spring. Gullies and big faces can be another matter. These should be carefully assessed for avalanche potential before venturing out onto them. Is there evidence of sluffing or sliding nearby? Are there tracks or runnels where snow has partially slid? Firm snow on a rubble slope alleviates the toil of an ascent and provides a glissade on descent, but too much snow may potentially avalanche once softened by the sun. Start early in the day in these conditions or, better yet, wait until the snow has melted. Wet snow avalanches occur largely during spring and early summer, and although they move slowly compared to powder snow and slab avalanches, they rapidly set up like concrete.

Elk and Bears

Few animals present a threat in the Rockies. The exceptions are moose or elk with calves, and bears, particularly if the bear has cubs. Keep your distance from any elk with a calf. Tourists in Banff can't seem to grasp this idea and almost yearly somebody gets charged or kicked by a protective mother.

Research has shown the human voice (e.g. singing, yelling) to be a better bear deterrent than bells or other noise makers. Stay alert and holler before coming over a rise or around a corner. An unexpected intrusion annoys most folks and bears generally have a very low tolerance for surprises. They are also a whole lot bigger than people! Making noise warns them of your presence and gives them a chance to steer out of your path.

When camping, hang anything smelling even remotely edible at least 4 m up a tree, or better yet, between two trees. Keep your camp clean and do not leave wash water or food bits around to entice bears. The cliché "a fed bear is a dead bear" says it all. Once they develop a taste for human food, they become a dangerous nuisance and are usually killed.

Watch for bear tracks and droppings along the trail. It doesn't take an expert to distinguish between types of bear scat. If it contains a bell, suspect a grizzly. Just kidding. Grizzlies do not stalk people as a source of food but will bluff charge or attack to eliminate a perceived threat, especially if they have cubs. This is when you may have to play dead. Curl up in a ball and cover your head and neck if possible. Grizzlies often attack and head and facial areas and leave the victim badly scarred both physically and emotionally. Extensive plastic surgery is often required to correct the damage.

Black bears, though smaller, can be very dangerous and have been known to stalk humans in a predatory manner. In a situation like this, you should be very aggressive. Yell, throw objects, and do whatever it takes to convince the beast that you are defending your territory and will not go without a good fight. Do NOT play dead in these circumstances, otherwise, you might be. Know how to identify each type. Grizzlies have a broader, dished face and a shoulder hump. Blacks are smaller, have a forehead "bump," and the shoulder is not humped. An excellent reference book is *Bear Attacks: Their Causes and Avoidance* by Dr. Stephen Herrero.

Many people venturing into the backcountry are arming themselves with an aerosol container of pepper-based spray in case of a bear attack. These cans fit in a holster that can be attached to your belt or pack strap. If a bear appears threatening, you calmly check wind direction so that neither you nor others will receive any of the debilitating spray, then carefully aim at the animal's face and shoot once it is within range. Easy, eh? The spray burns the eyes, rendering the victim near-helpless—temporarily. However, a panic-stricken human may not be thinking clearly enough to operate it correctly. From personal experience, it seems the busiest trails near most heavily populated areas (least likely to habour bears) will record the greatest crowds armed with bear spray.

Insects

These little pests are not hazards but are a definite nuisance. In the early season, wood ticks and mosquitos are the main complaint. Later, horseflies and small black flies take a turn. Bug repellents with an active ingredient called DEET are generally most effective, and some repellents now combine a sunscreen with an insect repellent. They do not include a perfume, though. Good bug lotions are smelly, sting your eyes, burn your lips, and can ruin plastics or synthetics if you're not careful.

In Canada, everyone has the right to bare arms. Biting insects are very happy when we exercise this freedom. Long-sleeved shirts, pants, gaiters, and a hat are effective deterrents against insects though, especially ticks. Wood ticks prefer hairy parts of the body. Finding and removing them by yourself can be a real trick. They have been known to carry Rocky Mountain Spotted Fever, but fortunately, this is extremely rare. Of more concern is the potential for them to carry Lyme disease, a progressive and debilitating condition affecting the nervous system. Ticks can be removed by gently tugging on them with a pair of tweezers. If bitten, consider saving the tick for analysis by medical people. This will be of considerable value if you experience any unusual symptoms like fever, a rash or ring around the bite, a headache or flu-like symptoms. Though not widespread right now, Lyme disease has been identified in at least two instances in western Canada so far.

Water

Ah, that beautiful fresh water. Well, not always, according to health officials. While I believe most water in the Canadian Rockies (or at least in the parks) is pure enough to drink right from the stream, the potential does exist for you to contract Giardia, also known as Beaver Fever. At this time, researchers in Calgary have developed a vaccine against this malady and are now seeking government approval for it. Until then, here's what it's all about.

Giardia is a protozoan parasite that can contaminate surface water and will make life very miserable if you are unlucky enough to ingest it. Symptoms can take up to 15 days to appear and include persistent diarrhea, cramps, weakness, and loss of appetite. It does not seem to run rampant despite what health officials suggest, but naturally, the closer you are to heavily used areas, the more likely you are to encounter it. Most backcountry folks I know drink from streams and have since the last ice age (well, almost). I know of nobody ever contracting the bug. Specific areas of the Rockies (Elk Valley, British Columbia, I believe) have reported cases, but generally, the higher up in the mountains you go, the smaller the risk. Furthermore, if everyone kept his dog out of the backcountry, the risk would remain small. Dogs and beavers are key carriers of the parasite, but everyone visiting the backcountry should dispose of human waste properly. Humans may carry the bug and may not realize it.

Here's how to dispose of human waste. Bury feces at least 15 cm (6 in.) deep and 60 m (200 ft.) from any water source. Above tree line and where soil is lacking, current thinking suggests using a flat rock and the smear technique to spread feces on other rocks. The sun's ultraviolet rays will then cause natural biodegradation, although toilet paper must be burned. If you use this smear technique, please do it well off the route and nowhere near the summit. UV is most intense (and effective) on the southwest aspect.

If you have any suspicions about the potability of your drinking water, there are a few choices for treating it. Most expensive is to purify it using a commercially available filter and pump, available at better outdoor stores. Boiling for 10 minutes will also to the trick. The simplest method is to use a purifying agent like iodine. Crystals are available, or use 4 to 8 drops of tincture of iodine (at pharmacies) per litre of water, shake well and wait 10 minutes. Adding a few drink crystals helps mask the resultant taste. Note that iodine will permanently taint the lining of some collapsible water bags, whereupon neither cheap wine, tomato juice, nor baking soda will remove the odour. Whew!

Avoiding Death by Scrambling

Scrambling can not only be hazardous to your life, but it can end it completely. Scrambling kills. Over the last few years, a typical scrambling accident has involved a young male from eastern Canada working a summer job in either Banff or Lake Louise. The person is full of energy and surrounded by impressive looking mountains but has no experience.

By distributing pamphlets to employers and displaying posters, Parks Canada has tried to inform this group in an effort to reduce future accidents. Unfortunately, the trend will probably continue, despite an abundance of information available. Still, information alone won't always keep you out of trouble. All the reading in the world is no substitute for experience, and it is not the intention of the author to suggest otherwise.

Undertaking any of the trips mentioned in this volume is a potentially HAZARDOUS ACTIVITY and COULD KILL YOU. Particular phrases used in route descriptions may lead the reader to believe that little danger or difficulty is involved. This is NOT true. Mountains are inherently dangerous and scrambling can be doubly dangerous. Participants are advised to go with caution and select a route within their level of ability and experience. If you're not sure what your abilities are, maybe you don't have any ability. Those without proper skills and experience should enroll in an appropriate course given by a recognized mountain school or Union Internationale des Associations d'Alpinisme (UIAA) approved mountain guide. I fully advocate appropriate training, however, you should keep one fact in mind: Many courses teach you the basic moves for moderate rock climbs, but few, if any, teach you how to **avoid** technical rock climbing. Avoiding technical rock climbing defines scrambling. Knowing the basics is important, but route-finding is a more important element to safe scrambling. In reality route-finding cannot be taught but is a skill that develops (hopefully!) over time.

Once you have proper training under your pack's belt, the next step is to go with experienced people. Clubs such as the Alpine Club of Canada bring climbers together and offer courses, group outings, and a chance to meet potential trip partners.

Anyone climbing in the mountains should strive to develop and refine their mountain skills and to rely less on the skill and judgment of others. As you do, your level of confidence and margin of safety will rise accordingly. That way, you will be less dependent on written route information and can make sound decisions on your own. DO NOT PUT UNBRIDLED FAITH IN THE INFORMATION CONTAINED IN THIS OR ANY OTHER GUIDEBOOK. Develop and use your own judgment, too. Persons following any advice or suggestions within these pages do so entirely at their own risk. The risk of scrambling is DYING. Be careful.

Additional Information

BY ANDREW NUGARA

Maps and GPS

A map of the area you will be scrambling/hiking in is essential. Unless you are already familiar with the route, it is strongly recommended that you take a good topographical map with you. Mark and I take a map on all trips, regardless of whether we are familiar with the terrain or not. You never know when you might want to take an alternate descent route or change your objective, and sometimes only a map that reveals the exact layout of the land will tell you if your new plans are feasible or not.

At present, there are two brands of maps available that are useful for these scrambles: NTS maps from National Resources Canada, which cover all areas of the Canadian Rockies and Gem Trek maps, which are specific to popular outdoor recreation areas. Both are available at Mountain Equipment Co-op and Maptown in Calgary, as well as other outdoor retailers. The following NTS maps are specific to this guidebook and should be in the possession of all who use routes within this book:

- 82 H/4 Waterton Lakes
- 82 G/1 Sage Creek
- 82 G/8 Beaver Mines
- 82 J/7 Mount Head
- 82 J/10 Mount Rae
- 82 J/11 Kananaskis Lakes
- 82 J/14 Spray Lakes Reservoir
- 82 J/15 Bragg Creek
- 82 O/3 Canmore

Most NTS maps have contour lines that represent 40 metres of elevation. For this reason, it is important that you not rely completely on the relative closeness of contour lines to choose a line of ascent or descent. An apparently low-angled route could be interrupted by a 20-metre vertical rock band, which will not show up on the map. In fact, rock bands of much greater elevation than the contour line interval will often not be indicated on topographical maps, especially when the surrounding terrain is low-angled. These maps are not water or tear resistant and so it is a good idea to carry them in a plastic bag.

Gem Trek maps provide another option for the majority of trips in this book. Most Gem Trek maps have contour lines that represent 25 metres of elevation and therefore contain a little more detail than their NTS counterparts. However, once again, you should be careful not to rely on these lines to make a judgment about a route. In truth, a map displaying that kind of detail simply doesn't exist at present. After all, a day of scrambling could come to an abrupt end upon reaching a vertical rock band of not more than 2 metres if there are no good hand or footholds—and there's no way a 2-metre rock band is going to appear on any map! Gem Trek maps are quite detailed and display maintained and unmaintained trails, official and unofficial peaks, and other points of interest. Many Gem Trek maps are water and tear resistant and therefore very durable. The following Gem Trek maps are very useful for ascents in this book:

- Waterton National Park
- Highwood & Cataract Creek
- Kananaskis Lakes
- Canmore and Kananaskis
- Bragg Creek

At the time of printing, there was no Gem Trek map available for the Castle area. Note: The red-lined map reproductions in this book are very general in nature and should be used in conjunction with the appropriate NTS or Gem Trek map.

Regardless of the brand of map you are using, it will show blue grid lines on the actual map and blue grid reference numbers on the sides of the map—the key to identifying a specific location on the map. On most maps, one square represents one square kilometre, though some may be two square kilometres. Grid reference (GR) numbers contain six digits. The first two indicate the west/east coordinate (located on the top and bottom of the map), and the third digit is an approximation of the distance east of the first two, with the square being divided into ten equal divisions (100 m each). For example, if the first three digits are 835, find 83 on the top or bottom of the map; the 5 indicates that the point you want is halfway (500 m) between 83 and 84. Digits four, five, and six operate in exactly the same way, but refer to the south/north coordinate on the sides of the map.

As we move to a paperless society, there is now the option to buy CD-ROMs that contain topographical maps. This enables you to zoom in on a specific area and print a small map just for that trip. This technology is still relatively new and some of the maps might not contain the detail you would like, however, improvements are being made every day and the aforementioned problem should soon be solved.

GPS (Global Positioning System) is a terrific complement to map reading and navigation. A GPS unit uses satellites orbiting Earth to triangulate the location of the unit. A good satellite signal can pinpoint your exact position to within one metre. It can also be used to track your progress (assuming you leave the unit on) and map out routes using waypoints. In white-outs and other scenarios where visibility has been severely compromised, GPS can be a godsend. A good connection, however, can sometimes be difficult to achieve in heavy cloud cover or when surrounded by trees, canyon walls, or other significant obstructions. For this reason—and others, such as dead batteries or malfunction of the unit—GPS should never be used as the only source of navigation. It is absolutely no substitute for good map-reading skills, use of a compass, and the ability to navigate with only a map and visual clues such as landmarks and the contours of the surrounding land.

GPS technology is presently advancing at an astronomical rate. Today's average unit will download detailed topographical maps that not only display major roads and landmarks, but also include contour lines, lakes, rivers, drainages, summits, back roads, trails, and much more.

Purists may balk at this new technology—or the use of any kind of GPS in the mountains for that matter—and their attitude certainly would not be misplaced. Over-reliance on GPS could land some people in serious trouble should they not also possess maps and good map-reading skills. Once again, it is imperative to reiterate that GPS **should not** replace the use of maps.

Note: for trips in this book, your GPS should be set to NAD 83 (North American Datum from 1983).

Note: For all red-lined photos, a dotted line indicates a section that is not visible. That is, the route is behind a visual obstruction; most often a rock wall.

Mountain Bikes

Like most of the trips in Kane's book, bike approaches are not feasible or permissible for the majority of the trips in this volume. There are, however, notable exceptions, and for many of the mountains in south Kananaskis that are on the Continental Divide, a bike is almost necessary. Most of these bike approaches are on old logging roads, which vary from smooth and gentle to steep and rocky. Often, you may encounter terrain that is awesome for bikes and terrain that is terrible for bikes on the same trail. In addition, the trails are often interrupted by river and creek crossings. Investing in a pair of hip-waders is recommended. You can do the entire approach wearing them, saving time and energy when you arrive at a crossing. The waders can then be left with your bike when that part of the trip is over. A pannier on your bike provides a good place to securely fasten your scrambling boots while you are riding.

Following are trips for which a bike is strongly recommended, as well as trips where it is suggested.

Strongly recommended:
- Vimy Peak/Ridge
- Mount Loomis via Loomis Creek Trail
- Mount McPhail
- Mount Muir
- Mount Strachan
- Mount Armstrong
- Threepoint Mountain

Suggested:
- Newman Peak
- Victoria Peak
- Victoria Ridge
- Mount Bishop
- Snow Peak
- Piggy Plus
- Wind Mountain
- Ribbon Peak
- Old Goat Mountain

River Crossings

I bring up this topic only because a number of scrambles in this book require the crossing of one of two major rivers in Kananaskis: the Kananaskis River and the Highwood River. The ford-ability of these two waterways can vary greatly according to the time of day, even the time of year, and can also be dependent on the amount of precipitation during the year.

The Kananaskis River can be especially tricky for the simple reason that its water level can vary greatly during the day. Water released from the dam at the Kananaskis Lakes can dramatically increase the level of the river from morning to evening. Even if the river is low in the morning, it may be dangerously high in the evening and may have to be re-assessed at that time. If necessary, be prepared to hike out via Stoney Trail and then back along Highway 40 to your vehicle.

Keep in mind that for ascents of Lorette, Skogan, and Mary Barclay, the river crossing can be avoided by hiking or biking Stoney Trail that starts from the Stoney Day Use area, about 1 km along the road to Nakiska ski hill.

Hip-waders are ideal for the above three ascents. For Lorette and Skogan, the parking area is no more than 50 metres from the river, and only a few hundred metres for Mary Barclay. Put the waders on at the car, cross the river and leave them on the other side for the return crossing. The water in this river is always painfully cold.

The Highwood River is less problematic than the Kananaskis River, but there is no way to avoid crossing it for Odlum, Loomis (via Loomis or Odlum Creek Trails), McPhail, Muir, Strachan, and Bishop. This river can be quite high in the spring and is best avoided then. In addition, many of the approaches mentioned above are best done on bike. Trying to get you and your bike across the Highwood safely can be especially dangerous when the water level is high. Once again, hip-waders are a great idea.

For ascents of Junction Mountain and Shunga-la-she, the Sheep River may also be impassable, especially in the spring. Having a back-up plan for all the ascents mentioned above (in case the river is too high) is always a good idea.

Winter Scrambling

Scrambling during the winter months or in winter conditions can often provide an infinitely more rewarding experience, both visually and aesthetically, than the same trip in summer. Of course, winter trips are also infinitely more dangerous and the appropriate training and knowledge are absolutely essential should you choose to venture out in winter conditions.

The line between scrambling and mountaineering can be a blurry one. Mountaineering usually implies glacier travel, including roped and often belayed climbing using snow pickets, ice screws, and other methods of belaying. These techniques are far beyond the scope of this book. Pick up the latest edition of *Freedom of the Hills*, or *The Mountaineering Handbook* by Craig Connelly to learn more about mountaineering, and seek training from a professional.

Winter scrambling—or perhaps more accurately, snow and ice travel that is not mountaineering—usually requires only an ice axe, perhaps crampons, and, of course, knowledge of how to use both. Learning how to self-arrest with an ice axe is a skill that no one travelling in the winter should be without. Self-arrest techniques can be learned from books, but they must be practiced so that they become intuitive and reflexive. If you have never practiced self-arrest, don't expect that you will be able to successfully execute one when required.

The ability to accurately assess snow conditions and avalanche potential are also skills imperative to safe winter travel. Even with those skills, many an experienced mountaineer or winter traveller has perished in an avalanche—very simply, avalanches are that unpredictable. Taking an avalanche safety course is absolutely essential. Wear an avalanche beacon, take a shovel and probe, and know how to use them. The best way to avoid being caught in an avalanche is to stay off and away from terrain that has the potential to slide. Again, this knowledge is best gained from taking a course—the meager fee for such a course could save your life. It may seem obvious, but travelling alone in suspect areas is downright foolish. Who's going to dig you out when you're lying helpless underneath a metre of hard-packed snow? And, as always, let someone know where you are going.

Although officially winter falls between December 21 and March 20, from a practical standpoint it can extend far beyond those limits. One can encounter winter-like conditions in any month of the year, however November to May are more reasonable guidelines than December to March. Location also plays an important role. As a general guideline, farther west means more snow. The Continental Divide holds snow far longer into the season than the front ranges do, and if you're looking for less or no snow, the eastern border is the place to go.

Mountains of the front ranges often make the best choices for winter ascents, primarily because, at any given time of the year, they can be relatively snow-free and have the lowest level of avalanche danger. Chinooks can quickly clear snow off these peaks, rendering them far less dangerous than their counterparts farther west.

Front range mountains are also the best choice when areas farther west are socked-in. It is not at all uncommon for heavy clouds to completely dissipate upon reaching the front ranges, granting clear skies to those in the area.

Those with cross-country skis or AT skis (a multi-purpose ski that can be used as a cross-country ski, heel free, or a downhill ski, heel locked in), and a modicum of skiing ability can also complete the approach (or the entire ascent) on skis. Again, ski mountaineering falls outside the scope of this book. Local ski mountaineering guru, Chic Scott, has written several excellent guidebooks on this subject.

Scrambling vs. Climbing

The line between scrambling and climbing is even more blurry than the one between scrambling and mountaineering. Some people can scramble up terrain that others will require a rope to ascend. Certainly, a traditional climber who regularly climbs 5.10 and above would more than likely be quite comfortable on low fifth-class terrain without a rope. Conversely, someone with very little experience could be completely out of their element on third-class terrain. This is where self-awareness and the ability to assess and critique your own level of climbing ability are so vitally important. Just because your best friend or some Joe Schmo in front of you scrambled easily up a steep section doesn't mean you should. A scramble for some might be a climb for others and vice versa.

Ego and pride can be your worst enemies in the mountains. Don't do anything that is clearly beyond your level of comfort, even if everyone else has done it. This seems obvious, but it's amazing what people will push themselves to do in favour of not appearing weak, nervous, or scared in front of their friends—better weak than dead!

Downclimbing is one of the true tests of scrambling ability. It is also the most consistent weakness of scramblers in general. A good friend of mine taught me a technique where you ascend a few steps and then downclimb it right away. Then climb higher and downclimb that section also. Repeat this process until you get to the top. Yes, it's time-consuming, but it's almost guaranteed that you'll have no problem downclimbing the whole section on return, and you'll improve your downclimbing confidence in the process. All the top-notch scramblers I know are also great downclimbers. If possible, find some time to practice this vital skill in a safe environment.

Scrambles in this edition (and also in Kane's volume) that receive the qualifier "a climber's scramble" do so for a very good reason. Any minor mistake or slip on one of these routes could very quickly **end your life**. If you are not comfortable with exposure, very steep terrain, loose rock, and difficult and exposed downclimbing, climber's scrambles are best avoided until you gain more experience and comfort with those situations.

Below is a list of the most difficult and dangerous of the scrambles in the book (in alphabetical order). Most of these scrambles not only involve steep and exposed scrambling, but also require a great deal of route-finding and decision making. As such, their route descriptions are more general in nature. For example, a detailed route description of Old Goat Mountain's East Ridge would not only be complicated and difficult to follow, but may also detract from the route-finding experience itself.

Scramblers who tackle the routes below should be confident in their abilities in all aspects of scrambling. For your own safety, it is also recommended that these routes be done in pairs or groups and avoided as solo trips. Ropes, harnesses, a small amount of climbing protection, and rappel gear would not be out of place in your pack.

- Mount Baldy (west ridge of West Peak)
- Mount Dungarvan
- GR628936 of "Lineham Creek Peaks"
- Mount Loomis (southern outlier)
- Mount Lougheed
- Old Goat Mountain
- Mount Richards

Helmets

Wearing a helmet simply makes sense. Increased use of helmets can be seen in a significant number of physical activities including biking, skiing, snowboarding, and roller-blading. There are two extremes: those who never wear a helmet and me! I've been known to put on the headgear even on the most simple and innocuous hike, and, of course, anything more involved means I bring a helmet and use it without question or hesitation.

Primarily, a helmet will protect your head should you fall, however, just as important is protection from objective hazards. The "rotten" Canadian Rockies come by that name honestly and rock fall from above is a serious concern. Most of the rock fall will unfortunately come from scramblers above who may accidentally dislodge rocks. At other times the "freeze-thaw" action of snow and ice will loosen sections of rock and send them hurling down the mountain, though this is more of a concern for mountaineering trips in heavy snowfall areas.

Slipping on scree or wet, loose rock, as well as general carelessness due to fatigue or complacency, are also good reasons to wear headgear. Helmets are neither heavy to carry nor uncomfortable to wear. They should be an integral part of your scrambling gear.

Rope

Carrying a rope is another issue that deserves some attention. By its very definition, scrambling (unroped climbing) precludes the use of rope. This, however, doesn't mean that a short length (10 or so metres) of 8 or 9 mm rope is out of place in your backpack. It will probably stay there on every one of your trips, but unforeseen circumstances may change the nature of a trip. Getting off route, a forced change of route, changing weather conditions, wet or icy rock, or a group member getting stuck on tricky and/or exposed terrain may make it necessary to use a rope as a last resort.

Learning how to use a rope properly (belaying, setting up anchors/protection, and rappelling) are all skills that require formal training. Take advantage of the relatively small fees charged for introductory rock-climbing courses and get some professional training. You will likely never use these techniques on any of the scrambles in this book, however, it is certainly comforting to possess the skills and know that you will be able to use them in unforeseen or emergency situations.

Unofficial, Unnamed, High Points, and GRs

You may have noticed that there are a few unnamed peaks in this book, especially in the Kananaskis area. Unnamed is not synonymous with "not worth ascending." The process and/or criteria for naming mountains can often appear to be arbitrary and illogical. For example, why are the five most significant high points of the Mount McDougall range all unnamed except for Mount McDougall? McDougall isn't even the highest point of the massif. Having ascended all of them, Mark and I agreed that the most interesting and gratifying was "Kananaskis Peak" at GR345444, not McDougall. Similar examples exist throughout the Rockies.

Don't deny yourself an enjoyable and worthwhile summit just because no one has chosen to give it an official title or it appears to be simply an insignificant high point of a larger mountain. After all, there are plenty of named and official summits out there, that really aren't worth a trip up. Also, it often really ly *is* the journey, not the destination.

The Seasons–Pros, Cons, and Preferences

Scrambling in the Canadian Rockies can be a year-round affair if you are so inclined. Here are some of the advantages and disadvantages of the different seasons.

Summer

Advantages	Disadvantages
Long days	Bears
Warm temperatures	Afternoon thunderstorms
No ticks	High water levels for river/creek crossings
Snow-free ascents (no avalanche danger)	Smoke from forest fires (depends on the year)
Bike approaches are possible	

Autumn

Advantages

Early snow enhances scenery

Fantastic lighting for early-morning photos

Low water levels for river/creek crossings

Comfortable hiking temperatures (not too hot or too cold)

Typically good weather and very few thundershowers

No ticks

Bike approaches are still possible

Larches changing colour

Disadvantages

Bears (berry season)

Winter

Advantages

Gorgeous winter scenery

Use of cross-country or AT skis is possible

Alpenglow

No ticks

No bears (no yelling to warn them)

Glissading

Disadvantages

Avalanche danger

Travel can be more strenuous/difficult

Cold temperatures and high wind-chill

Area closures, limited access

Short days

Spring

Advantages

Less snow for easier ascents and great scenery (late spring)

Disadvantages

Bears come out of hibernation

Ticks

High water levels for river/creek crossings

Area closures, limited access

High season for avalanches (February, March, and April)

Don't let the number of (or lack of) items in each column deter you from going out in any given season (specifically, spring). In my opinion, the single best advantage from all lists is the stunning scenery of winter—it's simply unbeatable!

Environmental Sensitivity

Admittedly, I feel a little hypocritical about addressing this subject since this guidebook promotes human activity in the mountains. In truth, our best means of exercising "environmental sensitivity" to the mountain environment is for all humans to simply get out and stay out—no residents, no tourists, no hikers, no scramblers, no climbers, no skiers—leaving the mountain environment to whom it belongs: animals and nature.

Nevertheless, that is a less than realistic ideal and therefore it is absolutely our obligation, as guests, to treat the mountain environment with the utmost care and respect. Here are a few general guidelines to follow when in the mountains:

1. Always use trails (whether animal or human) where they are available and don't shortcut over untouched terrain unless it is absolutely necessary.
2. Pick up garbage if you see it. Fortunately, garbage is not a serious issue in the Canadian Rockies right now—let's keep it that way.
3. Avoid interacting with any kind of wildlife—not just the obvious (bears, moose, etc.).
4. Avoid trampling over or damaging animal nests and other forms of animal dwellings.
5. Leave the mountain exactly as you found it—it should be as though you were never there.

On a personal note, one very positive side-effect of becoming a regular visitor to the mountains is that I have become far more cognizant of the planet's environmental concerns and therefore a more environmentally conscious person in the process. My consumption of resources has been dramatically reduced; I recycle everything I can; and I try to consider the environmental consequences of the activities I'm involved in. Hopefully, if we all do what we can to minimize our own negative impact on the environment, the mountains will continue to be a viable habitat for humans, animals, and plant life and will provide a clean, spectacular environment for all to appreciate and enjoy.

Scrambling Areas

Waterton

Waterton Park is one of my favourite areas of the Canadian Rockies: beautiful mountains, beautiful lakes, beautiful scenery, and unbelievable colours. The park also contains two of my favourite scrambles of the book: Mounts Dungarvan and Glendowan (Irish names, not Scottish, as is sometimes thought).

A well-used and well-maintained system of trails make access to most of the peaks quite easy and though you will probably run into other people on the trails, it is likely you will have the actual mountain to yourself. Waterton has become increasingly popular with hikers, sightseers, and tourists, but it is still relatively quiet when you leave the trails in search of a summit. Poor rock keeps climbers away and the disappearance of any glaciation means the area offers nothing for mountaineers. Never mind—that's all the more room for scramblers!

Mount Cleveland and Upper Waterton Lake provide a perfect background for the final push to the summit of Mount Richards.

One unpleasant aspect of the Waterton and Castle (next section) areas is ticks. Both areas are notorious for high populations of ticks from mid-March to July. There has been much discussion and controversy about their capacity to pass on Lyme disease to their hosts. Regardless of whether they carry the virus or not, it is best to check yourself thoroughly at the end of each trip and use the correct procedure for removing any unwanted intruders that have attached themselves to you. If a tick has been feeding on you, it may be prudent to keep it for testing after removal.

Geology

You will probably immediately notice a significant difference in the geology of the Waterton area compared to that of the Rockies farther north. The rock is primarily horizontally laid and the variety of colours of that rock is astounding. The horizontal bedding is explained by the Lewis Thrust. A few years ago (about 75 million, to be more exact), a huge slab of layered rock was thrust up in a northeasterly direction over the younger rock. For this reason, the rock in Waterton is some of the oldest in the Rockies. The slab was displaced a distance of approximately 100 km, ending up where Waterton, Glacier National Park, and much of their surrounding areas presently sit. This process took a mere 15 million years. Whereas most of the mountains of the Rockies were formed by thrust sheets being piled up against one another, the slab of the Lewis Thrust moved more or less as a single unit, causing the rock to maintain its horizontal orientation.

The horizontal bedding is certainly a benefit for scramblers, who will enjoy sections of terrific hands-on scrambling on a number of ascents (Mount Dungarvan definitely provides the best example). The step-like terrain often enables you to ascend areas that may appear to be too steep. Unfortunately, the quality of the rock is dismal, explaining the lack of rock-climbing routes in the area.

The colour of the rock in Waterton is arguably the area's best feature. Nowhere in the Canadian Rockies will you find such an amazing variety of rock and rock colours. The specific rock that is primarily responsible for this is argillite (the "g" is pronounced as a "j"). The argillite of Waterton comes mostly in two colours: red and green. Often they are seen together and it is not uncommon to see visually striking examples of alternating layers of red and green argillite. The rock is basically hardened mud. A small amount of iron in the rock is the cause of the unique colours: red, if the iron has been oxidized, and green, if not.

In addition to the argillite, various shades of brown, grey, and beige limestone and dolomite are also found in the Waterton area. The very distinctive band of black/dark grey rock—noticeable near and at the summits of Dungarvan, Glendowan, and many others—is an igneous rock, resulting from molten magma being injected between sedimentary layers. Put this variety of colourful rocks side by side and you're guaranteed a visual feast that simply can't be beat.

Climate and Weather

Chicago may be "The Windy City," but Waterton could certainly earn the title "The Windy National Park." The average daily wind speed in Waterton is 32 km/h, and speeds of up to 120 km/h are not uncommon. Wind gusts have been measured at a violent 150 km/h. You might want to stay well clear of cliff edges when the wind picks up. Before you leave home, check the weather forecasts, which often give high-wind warnings when applicable.

It may surprise you to find out that Waterton receives more precipitation than any other area in Alberta: an annual average of 1,072 mm, compared to 930 mm in the Columbia Icefields. April and June are the wettest and cloudiest months of the year. Average snowfall in winter amounts to 575 cm in the townsite.

Access

From Calgary: south on Highway 2, west on Highway 3 (toward Pincher Creek); south on Highway 6 to Pincher Creek. Turn left to remain on Highway 6 and drive about 50 km south. Turn right into Waterton Park. Park Pass required or can be purchased shortly after the turnoff.

Accommodation

The town of Waterton has several hotels and lodges, including the famous Prince of Wales Hotel. The townsite has one campground, and there are a few others in the area. Just before the turnoff to the park you'll find Waterton Springs Campground, and Crandell Campground (in the park) is ideal for any peaks along the Red Rock Parkway. Check for seasonal closures.

Waterton

Bellevue Hill	2,112 m	easy/moderate	page 29
Mount Dungarvan	2,614 m	difficult	page 32
Cloudy Ridge	2,607 m	moderate	page 36

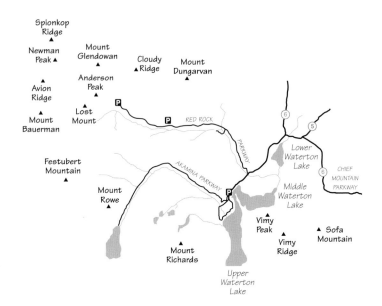

Mount Glendowan	2,677 m	moderate	page 40
Newman Peak	2,515 m	moderate	page 43
Spionkop Ridge	2,576 m	easy	page 45
Avion Ridge	2,440 m	easy	page 46
Mount Anderson	2,698 m	easy/moderate	page 46
Lost Mountain	2,509 m	easy	page 48
Mount Bauerman	2,409 m	easy	page 49
Mount Rowe	2,469 m	moderate	page 50
Festubert Mountain	2,522 m	easy	page 52
Richards	2,416 m	difficult	page 54
Vimy Peak/Ridge	2,379 m	moderate/difficult	page 57
Vimy Ridge	2,500 m	easy	page 60
Sofa Mountain	2,515 m	moderate	page 62

Bellevue Hill 2,112 m

Difficulty easy/moderate (depending on the route)
Round-trip time 3-5 hours
Elevation gain 750 m
Maps 82 H/4 Waterton Lakes, Gem Trek Waterton National Park

This "Hill" makes a great trip when time and/or energy are lacking or as an additional trip in conjunction with something close by when time and energy are in abundance. The colourful strata of the east face alone makes this a worthwhile trip. Red Rock Parkway is closed from November to mid-May. Try from June on.

Turn onto the Red Rock Parkway, drive for 3.5 km, and park at a small pull-off on the right side of the road. Check out the route (see photo). Hike along the road for an additional 100 m and ascend grassy, open slopes to reach the rock face. Traverse north alongside the face and pick one of two left rising

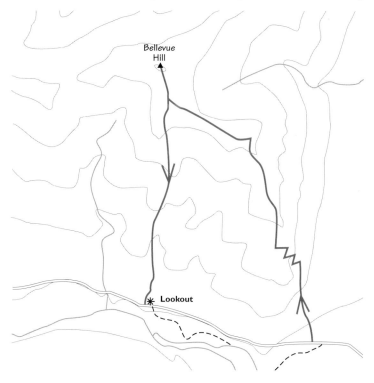

Ascent routes as seen from Red Rock Parkway. R ridge. C centre gully.

Route to the summit from the false summit. S summit. D easy descent route. G Mount Galwey.

ramps to gain higher slopes. Ascend one of the ramps and turn right, traversing wide ledges north and up. From here, your goal is to zigzag your way through colourful bands of rock toward the centre that splits the east face. You can gain the ridge at any point, but the most scenic and interesting route weaves its way almost to the centre gully and then the ridge just before it. Throughout, there are options to do easy, moderate, or difficult scrambling (be careful on the loose rock), whatever your preference.

Once you've gained the ridge, the fun is over. Turn right and try to enjoy the anticlimactic plod to the summit. The first major high point is a cairned false summit. The true summit lies 25 minutes away, to the northwest.

While the view may not be one of the most riveting you'll see, the pleasant contrast of grassy plains to the east, the Waterton Lakes and craggy peaks south of the border, and the familiar forms of Galwey and Blakiston to the west provides a uniqueness all its own.

The view to the southeast. Mount Cleveland in Glacier National Park dominates the horizon.

Either **return** the same way, or for a much faster descent, start south (the way you came), and instead of turning left toward the false summit, keep going south down the ridge. Trend left where it becomes obvious you must do so to maintain the ridge. Follow the ridge all the way down to the road, turn left and hike about 1.5 km back to your vehicle. This descent route can be completed comfortably in about 1.25 hours.

Mount Dungarvan 2,614 m

Difficulty Difficult via south ridge; exposed downclimbing;
a climber's scramble
Round trip time 8–11 hours
Elevation gain 1,160 m
Maps 82 H/4 Waterton Lakes, Gem Trek Waterton National Park

Mount Dungarvan could very well be the best scramble in Waterton National Park. The south ridge is a scrambler's dream of steep hands-on scrambling on step-like terrain. As well, the scenery throughout is fabulous. The summit block must be snow-free, so don't attempt it too early. If I could only do one trip in Waterton, this would be it. Red Rock Parkway is closed from November to mid-May. Try from July on.

Turn onto the Red Rock Parkway and park at the Lost Horse Creek parking lot. If the creek is low, it is possible to follow it along its banks to the start of the south ridge. Watch for two drainages coming down from the left. The second marks the start of the south ridge (approximately GR463825). Go past the second drainage and start up the ridge. Expect this approach to take approximately 2 hours.

If the creek is high (more than likely), it is better to side-slope on the left side of the creek. Again, look for the second drainage and head up the ridge after this drainage. Unfortunately, this option requires some nasty bushwhacking and climbing over endless deadfall. Again, allow 2 hours for the approach.

Once at the start of the south ridge, follow it up through thinning trees to the tree line. Here, the trip dramatically improves. For the next several hours, enjoy some of the best hands-on scrambling you're likely to find in the area. For the best bang for your buck, stay on the ridge to scramble up rock bands and pinnacles that may appear too steep for simple scrambling but are in fact very enjoyable to ascend. Although the rock is loose (typical of the area), its horizontal bedding inspires confidence, even when the rock quality doesn't. There may be at least one band that is too steep, however, it (and all others for that matter) can be easily circumvented on the left side.

Higher up, you arrive at a limestone rock band that is clearly not scrambling terrain. Again, traverse left along its base and then ascend one of numerous weaknesses. The farther left you go, the easier the ascent. Once above the band, head right and up to gain the ridge again.

Soon the summit block closes in: a band of black, lichen-covered rock atop a band of burgundy argillite (typical of several mountains in the area, like

Upper section of the south ridge. W weakness in rock band (approximate). G ascent gully. S summit. D easy descent route.

Summit block. G ascent gully. A alternate ascent route. S summit. D easy descent route.

Blakiston and Drywood). The argillite band is easily ascended, however, the black band can be a serious endeavour. If snow or ice persist on any of the potential ascent routes, this may become mountaineering, where rope skills—belaying, setting up anchors, rappelling—are imperative. If you are without climbing gear, be very cautious about ascending terrain that you may not be able to downclimb—"play it safe and retreat" is **always** the best policy.

If you're up for the challenge, traverse several metres on mildly exposed ledges around the right side of the summit block to a steep gully that grants access to the summit. If clear of snow and ice, this is your best bet. Otherwise traverse left along the base of the summit block and look for the easiest of several weaknesses. Even the least steep route (farthest left) requires steep scrambling and an exposed traverse along the final ridge to make it to the summit. Downclimbing either of these routes will require extra care.

Once at the top, enjoy a magnificent summit panorama before cautiously downclimbing (or rappelling) the summit block. When down, a fast and easier descent route exists by going straight down scree slopes of the south face of the mountain. Head far to the right to circumvent the limestone rock band and then continue down to the creek below. Follow the creek to where it joins up with Lost Horse Creek and then **return** the way you came.

The easier descent route. P parking lot. B Mount Blakiston.

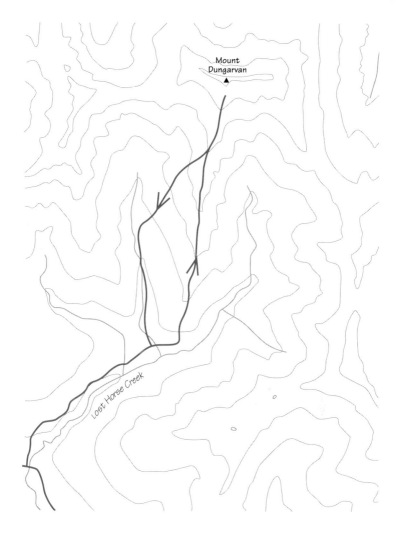

Mount
Dungarvan

Lost Horse Creek

Cloudy Ridge **2,607 m**

Difficulty Moderate via south ridge; mild exposure
Round-trip time 7–11 hours
Elevation gain 1,100 m + 400 m due to losses and regains
Maps 82 G/1 Sage Creek, Gem Trek Waterton National Park

Nestled between the two enjoyable south ridges of Dungarvan and Glendowan, Cloudy Ridge, unfortunately, falls short of its Irish cousins in terms of great hands-on scrambling. The scenery, however, is terrific and the final ridge and push to the summit is enjoyable in its own way. If you can stomach a necessary 200 m elevation loss on ascent (and then regain on descent) and a few sections of heavy bushwhacking, this is a good day out. Red Rock Parkway is closed from November to mid-May. Try from mid-June on.

The route from the parking lot. HP first high point. S summit.

Drive to the end of the Red Rock Parkway. From the parking lot, take a good look at the route in case you become entangled in the mess of deadfall and trees and want a quick escape to the ridge. The easiest route gains open slopes to the left of the creek and then traverses the ridge, descends to the creek, and crosses it. This puts you on the south slopes, where the route is obvious.

From the parking lot, cross the bridge that spans Red Rock Creek and turn right onto the paved trail. Hike the trail until you arrive at another bridge, which crosses to the other side. Don't cross. Hop the fence and continue on a good trail that parallels the creek. When the trail peters out, start heading left and up to open slopes, which you'll hopefully hit sooner rather than later. The bushwhacking here can be very tedious, as there is much deadfall.

Though gaining the ridge via the open slopes means gaining unnecessary elevation, it is considerably easier than trying to side-slope toward the south ridge of Cloudy, which leads to more difficult bushwhacking. Follow the ridge north until it starts to descend to a creek, about 200 vertical metres below. Here, it may be best to traverse left for a short distance until you reach an open slope that goes all the way down to the creek. As you descend, look for a good place to cross the creek and gain the open slopes of the beginning of the south ridge of Cloudy.

Once across the creek, trudge up grassy slopes to gain easy scree slopes. Soon, the route becomes visible. Follow the south ridge (along its edge for the best views and scenery) to the first high point. Turn left and traverse the burgundy-coloured ridge toward the summit. Pinnacles and rock bands on the ridge can be circumvented on either side or tackled head-on.

The route to the summit from the first high point. S summit.

Just before the summit, the vertical walls rear up to block the way. Downclimb a short step and look for a small col, down and a little to the right. Traverse down to it and then around the summit block (easy when dry, but you may feel a touch exposed if the route is snow-covered). Ascend up to a plateau that leads to easy terrain around and up to the summit. The farther you traverse around the block, the easier the terrain.

The summit is a flat and grassy plateau that is great for lounging around

The crux. C small col. S summit.

on and taking in the pleasant view. To the immediate east lies the slightly lower second summit of Cloudy Ridge. Dungarvan dominates to the southeast and Glendowan lies immediately northwest. As well, this is a great place to view many peaks of the Castle, Waterton, and Glacier National Park areas. **Return** the same way. Trying to avoid the necessary elevation gain by side-sloping on either side of Red Rock Creek means a good hour of difficult and strenuous bushwhacking—best to just bear down and ascend to the ridge again.

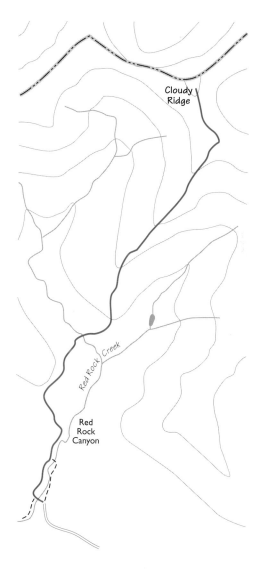

Cloudy
Ridge

Red Rock Creek

Red
Rock
Canyon

Mount Glendowan 2,677 m

Difficulty Moderate via southeast and south ridge
Round-trip time 7–10 hours
Elevation gain 1,175 m
Maps 82 G/1 Sage Creek, Gem Trek Waterton National Park

Mount Glendowan is very similar in nature to its easterly neighbour Dungarvan, but shorter and easier. The ascent features lots of hands-on scrambling and a tremendous variety of rock to keep things interesting. Scenery and views are terrific throughout. Except for a minor stint of tedious bushwhacking, this is an excellent day out. Red Rock Parkway is closed from November to mid-May. Try from June on.

The south ridge of Mount Glendowan, as seen from Anderson Peak.

Drive to the end of the Red Rock Parkway and hike the Snowshoe Trail for about 2.2 km to the first drainage (about 30–40 minutes at a moderate pace). Cross the creek (if it hasn't dried up) and turn right. Parallel the creek for several hundred metres. Climbing over deadfall may be tedious, but it could be way worse—just ask the British Columbians! You should now be at the start of the south ridge and, as long as you are going up and staying left of the creek, you should have no route-finding problems. The right side of the ridge offers occasional sections of relief from the bush.

Above the tree line, scree slopes lead easily to the start of the scrambling. The ridge is studded with interesting rock bands and pinnacles. To enjoy a fair dose of moderate to difficult scrambling, tackle them all head-on. Some are quite steep and the rock quality varies from decent to bad, so use good judgment—all can be circumvented on the left side. After some time, you may discover that the route is a little longer than anticipated and although staying on the ridge gives the most enjoyable ascent, it is also time-consuming. Move to the left if you feel the need to pick up the pace.

The upper slopes and summit block.

When the light shades of brown shale give way to the lichen-covered black band, look to the left of the ridge for an obvious, boulder-filled gully. Follow the gully up, trending to the left to avoid steeper terrain. The scrambling here should never be more than easy to moderate. At the top of the black band, regain the ridge to enjoy a stunning view of the lighter-coloured summit block. From this angle, the block appears intimidating, however, a short traverse (left about 50 m) along the base of the block reveals a weakness. Scramble up this weakness and ascend a scree slope to a high point. From there, it's a short and pleasant ridgewalk to the summit.

The summit view is first-rate in every direction. Of special interest are the beautiful hues and contours of the Castle Crown peaks to the north, Dungarvan (yet another terrific Waterton scramble) to the east, and a possible extension of the trip to the west, toward Newman Peak.

Return the same way. Once below the black band, it is possible to lose

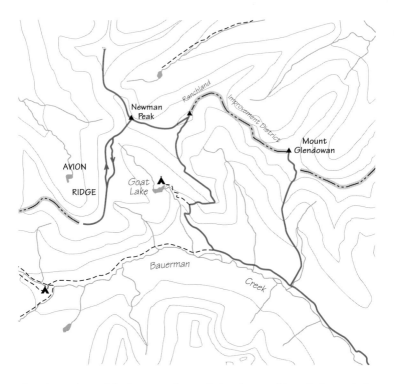

elevation quite rapidly down southwest-facing slopes. Although the creek far below looks like it may offer an easy route back to the Snowshoe Trail, the bushwhacking is quite bad, and therefore it is recommended that once you have lost enough elevation to circumvent the more serious rock bands of the ascent ridge, traverse left, back to the ridge and then follow the ascent route back to the trail.

Newman Peak 2,515 m

Difficulty Moderate with a few difficult, exposed steps
Round-trip time 6–12 hours
Elevation gain 1,000 m
Maps 82 G/1 Sage Creek, Gem Trek Waterton National Park

Newman Peak can be easily reached via popular hiking trails. A more interesting scramble route leaves the trail and ascends the southwest slopes. Once at the summit, there are plenty of opportunities to continue to other high points. Red Rock Parkway is closed from November to mid-May. Try from June on.

Park at the Red Rock Canyon parking lot and hike or bike 4.6 km along Snowshoe Trail to the Goat Lake sign. Leave your bike here and hike the Goat Lake Trail for several kilometres until it opens up, revealing the southwest slopes of the southeast outlier of Newman. The goal is to ascend these slopes to the outlier and then traverse the ridge northwest to Newman. Stay on the trail until it gets closer to the rock bands and look for a 10-metre scree ramp on the right that leads to an easy rock band. Start the ascent here, hiking up ledges and small rock bands and trending right as you gain elevation. WARNING: this route stays above the popular hiking trail for a long period of time. It is

The southwest ascent slopes from the Goat Lake Trail.

absolutely imperative that you DO NOT dislodge rocks onto unsuspecting hikers and backcountry campers below. Use extreme caution.

About two-thirds of the way up, the easy scrambling is interrupted by a smoother band of limestone. Traverse alongside it and ascend one of numerous weaknesses. Gain the upper ridge and go to the southeast outlier for a splendid view of Anderson, Blakiston, Glendowan, and the valley below.

The ridgewalk is probably the most interesting part of the ascent. Some sections look daunting, but generally this is an illusion. Stay on the ridge as much as possible. The odd pinnacle can be circumvented on the left. Near the end, the terrain becomes much steeper and the ridge narrows (recognizable by trees on the right side). Again, go around to the left and look for a moderate scrambling route to regain the ridge. Back on the ridge, you should see a huge near-vertical slab on the left side and treed terrain on the right. It is not necessary to descend to the treed terrain. Scramble up the right side of the ridge on exposed ledges to reach easier ground.

The southeast ridge. N Newman Peak. U higher unnamed high point. C Newman/Avion col. A route to Avion Ridge. D easy descent trail.

At this point, a higher and unnamed bump to your right is closer to Newman's Summit and you should head there for a quick look. Otherwise, sideslope, trending left to the summit of Newman. From the bump, take in the pleasant view and then go west to Newman.

From the summit of Newman there are several options to extend the day, which are listed below. If **returning**, do not use the ascent route—it will be more difficult to avoid knocking down rocks going *down* the southwest slopes. Instead, descend the west ridge of Newman to the col a few minutes away.

Here, a well-travelled trail heads down into the valley and arrives at Goat Lake. The trail then continues down, and soon you'll arrive at the place where you left the trail on ascent.

Spionkop Ridge 2,576 m

The shortest and most interesting extension of the Newman Scramble goes north to the summit of Spionkop Ridge. No difficulties. Looking down the length of Spionkop Ridge and Loaf Mountain to the north will be a good reward for the extra effort. If you're feeling really energetic, you can continue north to reach the summit of Loaf Mountain quite easily. This, however, leaves you a great distance from your car and is recommended only if you can travel fast and have plenty of daylight for the long return trip.

Extension to the north from Newman Peak. S Spionkop Ridge. L Loaf Mountain.

Avion Ridge 2,440 m

A second option from Newman goes southwest to the summit of Avion Ridge. Descend southwest to the col, where a trail curves around the west side of the ridge. If time is a concern, follow that trail—it goes all the way to the summit. A more scenic route stays on the ridge and then joins up with the trail as you descend southwest from the ridge and then on to the summit. **Return** the same way.

Mount Anderson 2,698 m

Difficulty Easy to moderate via south slopes or southeast ridge
Round-trip time 5–8 hours
Elevation gain 1,200 m
Maps 82 G/1 Sage Creek, Gem Trek Waterton National Park

At 2,698 m, Mount Anderson is one of Waterton's taller peaks. The route described here is more or less a steep hike, but there are options to take more challenging routes to the summit. Continuing west to Lost Mountain and then to Mount Bauerman makes for a wonderfully scenic and interesting day out. Red Rock Parkway is closed from November to mid-May. Try from June on.

Start at the Red Rock Canyon Parking lot and follow the signs to Blakiston Falls. Continue on the trail past the falls for approximately another 4 km (approximately one hour from the parking lot at a moderately fast pace). Check to the right now and then, looking for an obvious grassy slope that leads

Anderson, Lost, and Bauerman, seen from Blakiston. A Anderson. C Anderson/Lost col. L Lost. B Bauerman. AD alternate descent.

easily to the Anderson/Lost col (a waterfall and drainage bisect the slope). This slope is quite foreshortened and may take longer than you anticipate. Traverse to the right side of the slope to gain a better view and then just head up the ridge. Follow it to the summit.

The top offers a great view of the scramble routes up the south ridges of Glendowan and Dungarvan, as well as the north side of Blakiston. After enjoying the typical fare of extraordinary Waterton colours seen from the top, either **return** the way you came, or head back down to the col and then continue west, up interesting step-like terrain to the summit of Lost Mountain (20–30 minutes from Anderson to Lost). You may need only a minute or two

Easy route to the Anderson/Lost col.

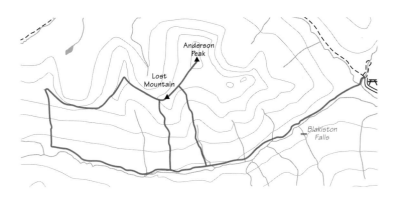

to catch your breath and take a few pictures before continuing the pleasant and stress-free trip toward Mount Bauerman (not visible from Lost). If Bauerman is not on the agenda, **return** to the Anderson/Lost col, then turn right and descend easy slopes back to the Blakiston Creek Trail.

Lost Mountain 2,509 m

Difficulty Easy via south slopes
Round-trip time 5–9 hours
Elevation gain 1,000 m
Maps 82 G/1 Sage Creek, Gem Trek Waterton National Park

Though best combined with an ascent of Mount Anderson and/or Mount Bauer-man, Lost Mountain offers an easy scramble, with interesting scenery along Blakiston Creek and a decent summit view, and is therefore worthwhile by itself. Nabbing Mount Anderson adds only an hour to Mount Anderson and heading west to Mount Bauerman a couple more, though the trip from Lost to Bauerman is the most interesting and scenic part of the trip. Scrambling Lost Mountain is a pleasant day with options for one, two, or three summits. Mostly steep hiking. Red Rock Parkway is closed from November to mid-May. Try from June on.

There are two easy routes to the summit of Lost, both starting at Red Rock Canyon parking lot. If you are planning to also summit Mount Anderson, see

Direct route to the summits, seen from Blakiston Trail.

the route description for Anderson. Once at the Anderson/Lost col, turn right to the summit of Anderson or left for the summit of Lost.

The second route goes more directly to the summit of Lost, although it may be a little longer than the first route. Start at the Red Rock Canyon parking lot and follow the signs to Blakiston Falls. Continue on the trail past the falls for approximately 5 km (about 1.25 hours from the parking lot at a moderately fast pace). Check to the right now and then, looking for an obvious grassy slope that leads easily to the summit block of Lost. As soon as you see it, turn right through light bush and gain the open slopes. Be careful not to overshoot this key point, as you may end up in some fairly dense forest when you turn right. The grassy slopes soon give way to annoying treadmill scree, where you'll probably want a set of hiking poles. As you gain elevation, trend a little to the left. Near the top, the steep and loose summit block can be easily circumvented on the left side. Once on the ridge, turn right and continue up gentle slopes to the summit.

The view is very pleasant, even though the taller Mount Anderson blocks some of the panorama—a good excuse for you to run over to that summit (only a one-hour round trip). Hopefully, the beautiful red argillite slopes of the unnamed peak to the west will catch your attention and motivate you to continue on to it and then to Mount Bauerman. If not, **return** the same way.

Mount Bauerman 2,409 m

To get to Bauerman, you must first gain the higher unnamed peak between Lost and Bauerman by dropping down to the col and then re-ascending the wonderfully scenic rock to the summit—arguably the best part of the entire day. Unless the characteristically fierce Waterton wind is howling from the west, stay near the edge throughout to enjoy vertiginous views down the north side and more fantastic rock.

At the summit, Bauerman comes into view and it may look to be quite far away at this point in the scramble! Thankfully, the terrain is easy and enjoyable to negotiate, and the grade is so mellow you'll hardly even know you're going up. As well, the scenery changes nicely as you reach the low point and make your way through trees lining the col. Again, the vertical north face of Bauerman provides an impressive diversion as you decide whether your legs are going to get you back to the car after all this.

A well-worn trail takes you all the way to the summit, where a puny cairn and respectable summit view await. Although you can **return** the same way, a far easier and less strenuous option is to descend scree slopes heading south directly from the summit. Trend a little left as you rapidly lose elevation on very surfable scree. The scree eventually gives way to grassy and treed slopes.

Keep heading down, picking the easiest line with the least amount of trees. Eventually you'll run into Blakiston Creek Trail. Turn left onto the trail and enjoy the 9-km hike back to your car. Make sure you don't walk right by some of the terrific scenery of Blakiston Creek, including stunning red and green argillite rock.

Mount Rowe 2,469 m

Difficulty Moderate via southeast slopes; some exposure if northeast ridge is followed
Round-trip time 4.5–6 hours; add 2–8 hours if extensions are taken
Elevation gain 800 m (Rowe only)
Maps 82 G/1 Sage Creek, Gem Trek Waterton National Park

What Mount Rowe lacks in height, it makes up for in strategic location and versatility. The trip can be completed in less than 4 hours or one can make a full day of it, with multiple extension possibilities and/or a return route via the scenic Rowe Lakes. Try from July on.

The ascent route from the road. CD centre drainage. NR northeast ridge.

Park at a pull-off on the right side of the road 13.1 km along the Akamina Parkway (right by the winter gates). Walk about 150 m farther down the road, looking for a small, dried-up drainage on the right. This drainage is the key to the ascent and leads almost all the way to the summit. Hike up the drainage, moving to the left or right side when vegetation takes over the path. Whenever possible, stay in the drainage to enjoy some easy but enjoyable hands-on scrambling.

Vegetation takes over again, and, as you gain elevation, the upper slopes and summit of Rowe appear to the left. Move back into the drainage and stay there, making your way easily up the southeast slopes. As you approach the middle of the southeast face, there are two ascent options.

The first option is moderate scrambling up the centre of the face. Continue up the drainage until another drainage comes in from the left and runs right up the middle of the face. This drainage goes right in between two prominent uplifts of rock to the summit.

The second option is a scree slog followed by an exciting ridge scramble to the summit. Continue up the drainage as it swings to the right and then becomes a scree slope, leading to the ridge and skyline right of the summit. Once on the ridge, follow the crest up increasingly narrow and exposed terrain to the summit. The scrambling here is never difficult, but do remind yourself of the quality (or lack of it) of the rock you are ascending. All too soon the scrambling ends as you arrive at a cairned false summit. A short hike leads to the true one.

Upper ascent routes. CD centre drainage. NR northeast ridge.

The summit view is quite impressive, though, needless to say, most of the surrounding mountains are taller than the summit you're on. The Upper Rowe Lakes look particularly inviting from this summit—as do the taller peaks south of the border—and impressive colour contrasts of light brown Lineham, red Hawkins, and the greenish outlier to the left of Hawkins make this view notable. Mount Festubert lies farther northwest.

Numerous options and extensions are available when you are ready to continue.

You could simply return the same way.

Or, return via the Rowe Lakes Trail. Descend the northeast ridge until it becomes possible to drop down to easy slopes on your left. Traverse down and northeast, arriving quickly at the Upper Rowe Lakes. Find the trail at the north end of the second lake and follow it for 6.4 km to the trailhead. Turn right and hike 2.6 km back to your car.

As a third option, you could return by continuing west and then north along the Rowe ridge to an unnamed high point at GR136374. The view of the lakes continues to improve the farther along the ridge you travel, and eventually distinctive Festubert Mountain comes into view to the northwest. Also note the grassy bump that allows you to escape to the Upper Rowe Lakes without having to return to Mount Rowe. From the summit at GR136374, the next high point at GR133382 is only worthwhile if you intend to continue all the way to Festubert. Better just to relax, take in the view, and then either return the way you came or make your way down to Upper Rowe Lake via the aforementioned "grassy bump."

Festubert Mountain 2,522 m

Add 400 m of elevation gain. 8.5-11 hours for both mountains.

If you plan to scramble Festubert Mountain at any point, this is the time, given that the best route to the summit traverses the entire ridge from Mount Rowe. The route barely needs a description—from Mount Rowe, follow the ridge in a northwest direction until you get there! There are two major high points along the way, both of which surpass Mount Rowe in height GR136374 and GR133382. It is worth visiting both, but if you wish to avoid the extra elevation gain, side-sloping the second high point is possible. The remainder of the ridge is sparsely treed and the most enjoyable route follows faint trails alongside the edge. The final push to the summit can be tackled along the ridge edge (a couple of sections of moderate to difficult scrambling), or via easy scree by traversing left around the rock bands. The summit view probably won't take you by storm, as it's basically what you've been looking at for the past three hours.

Festubert Mountain from the first high point. F Festubert. HP second high point.

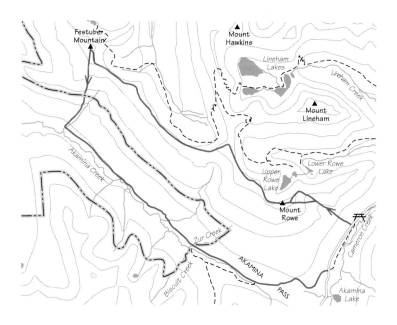

Either **return** the same way (taking into account that this return will add another 350 m of elevation gain to your day), or use the south slopes as follows: descend the way you came for a few hundred metres, looking for the obvious scree slope on your right that goes most of the way to the valley bottom. Head down those slopes, enjoying several hundred vertical metres of excellent scree-surfing. Trend left a little as you descend. Soon the slope narrows into a drainage that can be followed all the way down to the Westside Road (trail). Expect a short, but nasty stint of bushwhacking alongside a creek. Once you arrive at the trail, turn left and enjoy a mind-numbing 11-km hike to the Akamina Pass Trailhead. Another 1.5-km hike north along the Akamina Parkway completes a long day.

Mount Richards 2,416 m

Difficulty Difficult, steep, and exposed scrambling via north ridge and southeast ridge; a climber's scramble
Round-trip time 11–14 hours
Elevation gain 1,500 m (includes necessary losses)
Maps 82 H/4 Waterton Lakes, Gem Trek Waterton National Park

For a diminutive mountain, Richards packs a real punch. Although there are easier and faster routes to the summit, the one described here is long, physically demanding, and requires much route-finding and exposed scrambling. Thank-

The north ridge, seen from Bertha Peak. C Mount Cleveland. F false summit.

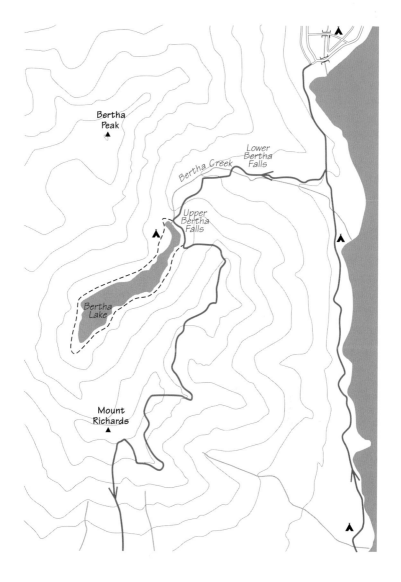

Bertha Peak

Lower Bertha Falls

Bertha Creek

Upper Bertha Falls

Bertha Lake

Mount Richards

fully, an easy descent route rewards those who persevere to the summit. Note: the easiest descent route requires you to briefly cross into the United States. Be sure you are carrying proof of citizenship if you choose to take this route. Try from July on.

Drive into Waterton and follow Evergreen Avenue to a gravel parking lot on the right, the Bertha Lake trailhead. Hike 5.2 km to Bertha Lake. Continue around the east side of the lake on the lakeshore trail for about 5 minutes. When it becomes obvious, take a sharp left and head up the ramp alongside the tree line aiming for the point on the north ridge where the tree line ends.

For the next several hours, enjoy the challenge of scrambling the north ridge. At times, it is necessary to lose elevation and circumvent steep rock bands on the right side, but always try to return to the ridge for the best scrambling and fantastic views of Upper Waterton Lake, backdropped beautifully by Mount Cleveland. Route-finding can be a challenge, and often you will be required to scramble up steep, exposed terrain. On the way, there are several high points where you can rest and enjoy the scenery. Expect your horizontal progress toward the summit to be very slow.

Eventually, you'll arrive at a high point before a low col, followed by a striking ridge of red argillite. Quite obviously, continuing along the north ridge at this point would require technical climbing. Drop down to the col and follow a good trail on the east side. The argillite rock bands along the way are stun-

The final section from the false summit.

ning. Re-ascend to a col on the other side (the east ridge), and then turn right and ascend easy slopes to a false summit. This is not a necessary elevation gain, but the scenery is worth the effort. Also, if you choose to cut the trip short, from the false summit you can descend slopes to Bertha Lake and then out.

At the false summit, it is again disheartening to find the ridge too steep to scramble. Again, you must lose elevation on the east side of the mountain and traverse steep-looking slopes over to the southeast ridge. Once on the southeast ridge, the summit is now close but requires more steep scrambling and route-finding. One route ascends the ridge until the rock band forces you left and down into a gully. Ascend this gully until it tops out, then turn right and regain the ridge. A short scramble gets you to the summit. The summit view is incredible: Bertha Lake and Mount Alderson on one side, and Upper Waterton Lake and an array of spectacular peaks south of the border on the other.

Two alternate descent routes exist. Easiest is down the south slopes and out via the Boundary and Waterton Lakeshore trails. Either descend easier slopes to the southwest, swinging around to the left and back onto the original slope when the cliff bands to your left run out, or descend the ascent route, which takes you directly onto the main descent slope. Find the Boundary Trail, just before the creek at the bottom, and turn left. Hike the trail for several kilometres. Turn left again when it intersects with the Waterton Lakeshore Trail and follow the trail 6.4 km back to the parking lot. Again, a reminder that you must carry proof of citizenship for this alternate descent route.

The other descent route retraces the ascent route until back at the east ridge. It is then possible to drop down into the valley north of the ridge and descend east out to the Waterton Lakeshore Trail. Turn left and hike easily back to the parking lot. This route requires a little more energy, but it does avoid having to cross into the United States.

Vimy Peak/Ridge 2,379 m

Difficulty Moderate with one difficult, but avoidable rock band
Round-trip time 7–9 hours for peak; add 5–7 hours for ridge
Elevation gain 1,100 m for peak; add 500 m for ridge
Maps 82 H/4 Waterton Lakes, Gem Trek Waterton National Park

Though the summit of Vimy Peak can be reached by a long but straightforward hiking trail, a more interesting route tackles the scenic north side more directly and is described here. The hiking trail then makes for an easy descent. Continuing on to the high point of Vimy Ridge will truly put your stamina to the test. Take twice as much water as you think you'll need, as well as a headlamp. Try from mid-June on.

Ascent route from the clearing. D difficult route to the ridge. E easy route.

Drive to Pincher Creek and keep heading south on Highway 6. Turn right (still on Highway 6) 900 m after passing the turnoff to Waterton Park. Drive 500 m and park at a pull-off on the left side of the road (Wishbone Trailhead sign on other side of the road). Hike—or better yet, bike—the Wishbone Trail for 7 km (5.5 km to the Sofa Creek crossing and then 1.5 km to junction). This trail is very narrow. Make lots of noise, not only to warn wildlife, but also to alert other people on the trail.

Leave your bike at the signed junction, even though bikes are permitted on the Wishbone Trail—you'll be using the easy descent route and the junction is where you'll end up. Take the right fork (Wishbone Trail) at the junction and continue on foot until you reach an unusual clearing scattered with dead trees. Turn left up this clearing, aiming for a rocky drainage at the back right side. Ascend the middle of the drainage. It is possible to continue up the entire drainage, however, a more interesting route gains the ridge to the right when a prominent band of alternating layers of light brown and greenish rock appears on the right side. Scramble up this band to reach the ridge, where a good view of the Waterton lakes awaits. Moderate scrambling up this ridge leads to a rubble slope below Vimy's impressive, vertical north face. Aim for a prominent notch at the left side of the face. This area provides access to the summit ridge by a weakness through the rock band.

At the base of the weakness, assess the terrain. It is steep and involves difficult and exposed scrambling for the first several metres. If not to your liking, continue east to circumvent the band entirely. The best route up the band is right up the middle on small ledges. The rock is generally solid and a few good handholds make life easier. Trend right to easier terrain and then continue up. The towering pinnacles of rock are well worth a visit. Gain the ridge and continue to the summit.

As expected, the view of the Lower and Middle Waterton Lakes and the surrounding peaks is great, but most of the Upper Lake is out of view. Continuing west to a lower summit on the ridge allows a glimpse of the Upper Lake, and it is still a worthwhile and scenic diversion. If satiated, either **return** the same way or take a slightly longer but easier route via the Vimy Peak Trail. The trail heads southeast down the peak and then into the treed valley between two ridges. The distance for this return is 5.8 km from the summit to Wishbone/Vimy junction.

Preparing to ascend the difficult route to the ridge.

Vimy Ridge 2,500 m

The long ridgewalk to the highest summit of Vimy Ridge at GR939323 is easy but leaves you a great distance from your car (a solid 18 km if you go to the highest point). Ensure your water supply is plentiful and start down the ridge in a southeast direction. Stay on the crest of the ridge throughout. At the first high point, it is easy to bail out and go north down to Vimy Basin and the trail—a popular option for many hikers. Otherwise, keep going and going. The lakes quickly disappear behind other peaks, but the view toward Crypt Lake and Mount Cleveland to the south improves with each several hundred steps!

Technically, the summit of the ridge lies at GR929331, with an elevation of 2,416 m. The highest and most scenic summit, however, is the next point to the southeast. If you've made it to the first summit, you might as well finish the job. At GR939323, pat yourself on the back, enjoy the view, and then **return** the same way, using the alternate descent down the Vimy Peak Trail (see above). It is possible to avoid too much elevation regain by side-sloping the east side of the mountain, but the travel may be slower and self-defeating. DO NOT try to shortcut by descending into the valley north of GR939323 and then directly to the southeast leg of Sofa Creek (unless you're carrying a 300-m rappel rope!).

The route to Vimy Ridge and beyond. B bailout route. VR summit of Vimy Ridge. HP high point of the traverse. C Mount Cleveland.

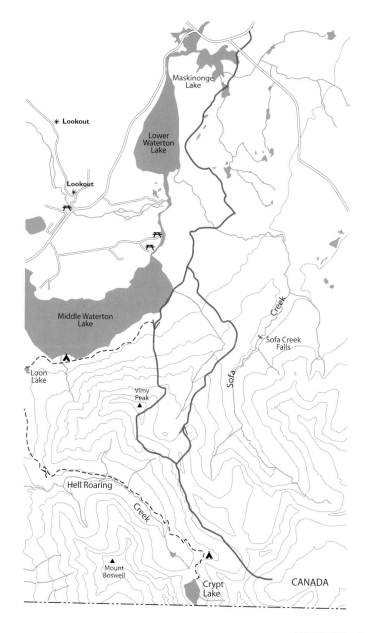

Sofa Mountain 2,515 m

Difficulty Moderate via the northeast ridge
Round-trip time 6–8 hours
Elevation gain 900 m
Maps 82 H/4 Waterton Lakes, Gem Trek Waterton National Park

The northeast ridge of Sofa Mountain offers about 20 minutes of excellent scrambling on solid rock. A good trail takes you quickly and easily to the mountain and on a clear day, the views to the west and southwest are terrific. Try from June on.

The ascent route, as seen from a few hundred metres east of the start of the trail.
AD alternate descent.

Drive toward Waterton, but do not turn right into the park. Instead, continue on Highway 6 for about 1 km and turn right onto Highway 6 South (Chief Mountain Parkway). Drive for 7.3 km and park at a gravel pull-off on the right side of the road. The trail starts here. Hike the trail, as it wanders up and over hills, through light forested terrain and grassy meadows in a southerly direction. In about 45 minutes you'll arrive at the foot of the northeast ridge. The trail continues west, heading toward the valley between the northeast ridge and its southerly counterpart.

Instead of following the trail into the valley (use this route on descent), head directly up steeper, grassy slopes of the northeast ridge. At the top, the rest of the ridge and the route up it become clear. Hike up scree slopes to the

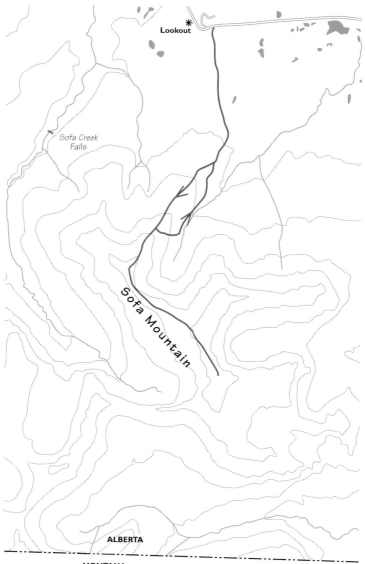

Lookout

Sofa Creek
Falls

Sofa Mountain

ALBERTA

MONTANA

Arriving at the base of the mountain.

start of the scrambling. Scramble straight up the first rock band. If it is too steep, traverse left for a short distance and ascend an obvious gully. The rock is solid, with good hand- and footholds. Continue up the ridge by tackling all rock bands head-on or slightly to the left, depending on your preference.

At the top of the northeast ridge, turn left and hike easily for 2 km to the summit. The summit panorama includes Chief Mountain and Mount Cleveland, two of Glacier National Park's more distinctive peaks, as well as a comprehensive view of most of Waterton Park. **Return** the same way. Once below the scrambling section of the northeast ridge, turn right and hike down into the valley below. Follow the stream out, taking in a couple of scenic waterfalls along the way. Find the trail that takes you back around to the base of the northeast ridge and follow it out.

The Castle

The stretch of land north of Waterton National Park is one of the best-kept secrets in the Canadian Rockies (until now, I suppose!). I would not have known about it if not for the insight and adventurous nature of Linda Breton, who introduced me to the Castle area and a number of ascents within its borders. Host to many interesting scrambles, the area sees little traffic and more than likely you will have the mountains all to yourself. Like Waterton, its neighbour to the south, the variety of rock and rock colours are the highlights of the Castle area. Eye-catching bands of red and green argillite are features of most peaks. As well, there are numerous trail systems that make access and approaches to scrambles considerably easier. Some of these trails are well-suited for mountain bikes.

The area—also called the Castle Crown and Castle Wilderness—encompasses approximately 1,000 square km of land and is about twice as big as Waterton. The diverse ecology of the Castle is remarkable: aspen parklands, fescue grasslands, montane and sub-alpine forests, alpine meadows, hanging valleys, and high elevation lakes make up the area. The Castle is also home to an incredible variety of plant life, including approximately 120 rare species

The sun lights up a lenticular cloud formation on the way to Victoria Peak.

(about three times as many as are found in Banff National Park). Animal life is equally diverse. Bears, ungulates, wolverines, cougars and wolves, to name a few, are common to the area and use it as a corridor to other areas to the south and west.

Unfortunately, the land does not lie within the boundaries of a national or provincial park, and therefore does not enjoy the environmental protection afforded to areas that do. Perhaps more than any other area in the book, preservation of this pristine environment requires special attention from each of us. Environmental groups are presently working to ensure that logging, clear-cutting, mining, and oil and gas extraction do not irreparably damage this delicate and precious environment.

Autumn is often the best time of the year for ascents in the Castle. The stunning array of rock colours are still visible, the larches are changing colour, early snowfall can enhance the beautiful scenery even more, creek crossings are easier, and ticks are not an issue. Of course, unless you are lucky enough to live in the area, you might be making breakfast at 4 am and leaving the city at 5 am in order to get to the trailhead early enough.

Geology

The geology of the Castle is much the same as that of Waterton. See p.26 for details.

Climate and Weather

Like Waterton, the Castle area is subject to very high winds. This can be a double-edged sword. Those high winds can clear west-facing slopes of snow early in the year, making this a good area for early-season trips. Of course, being on a peak during high-wind periods can be dangerous. Gusts of up to 100 km/h are not uncommon in this area and can easily knock you off your

A panorama of the Front Range peaks of East Castle.

C Mount Cleveland. D Mount Dungarvan. CR Cloudy Ridge. R Mount Roche.

feet. Avoiding exposed scrambling situations is strongly recommended when the wind picks up. Before you leave home, check the weather forecasts, which often give high-wind warnings when applicable.

Access

From Calgary: south on Highway 2, west on Highway 3 (toward Pincher Creek); south on Highway 6 to Pincher Creek. For peaks in the West Castle area, turn right onto Highway 507. For peaks in the East Castle area continue south (turning left to remain on Highway 6), through Pincher Creek and toward Waterton.

Accommodation

The town of Pincher Creek has a number of motels and hotels. For less luxurious accommodations, there are quite a few campgrounds close to the town. If you want to get a little closer to the mountains, there are campgrounds at Beauvais Lake (off Highway 507) and Beaver Mines Lake (off Highway 774), as well as several others in the area. Check for seasonal closures.

East Castle

Victoria Peak	2,587 m	moderate	page 70
Victoria Ridge	2,530 m	easy	page 72
Pincher Ridge	2,423 m	difficult	page 74
Drywood Mountain	2,514 m	moderate	page 77
Loaf Mountain	2,640 m	easy	page 80
Mount Roche	2,492 m	moderate/difficult	page 82

L Loaf Mountain. DR Drywood Mountain. P Pincher Ridge. V Victoria Peak.

The summit block of Mount Roche.

The peaks in this section all lie in the Front Ranges and are readily viewed when driving south on Highway 6, between Pincher Creek and Waterton. Though not particularly striking from a distance, these mountains are absolutely beautiful up close. Pincher Ridge has a rock band that displays one of the most impressive examples of multicoloured rock layering I've ever seen. A little farther to the northwest sits Victoria Ridge, perhaps one of the best ridgewalks in the Canadian Rockies. You are unlikely to find another ridge whose views boast such an amazing variety of colours. Every peak in this section offers not only visual spectacles that are guaranteed to impress and delight but also a fair amount of decent hands-on scrambling. The rock quality is a little suspect, as expected, but then you can't have everything, can you?

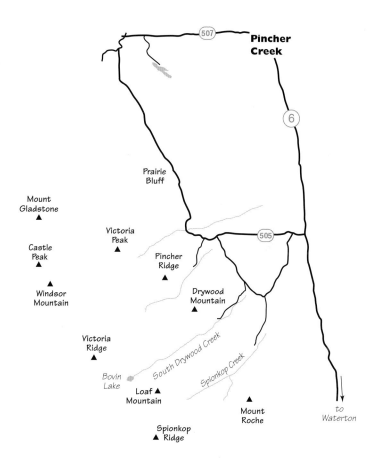

Victoria Peak 2,587 m

Difficulty Moderate via southeast slopes
Round-trip time 4–7 hours
Elevation gain 1,100 m
Maps 82 G/8 Beaver Mines

Victoria Peak is a thoroughly enjoyable scramble, best done in fall when the larches are changing colour. On a clear day, the variety of colours you'll see are worth the trip. There is also the option to extend the trip to Victoria Ridge for a full and colourful day. Try from mid-June on.

The ascent and descent routes from the approach trail. ED easier descent.

From Pincher Creek, head south toward Waterton. About 20.5 km south of the south end of Pincher Creek, take Highway 505 west (the east turnoff comes up first—don't take it!). Follow the 505 for 9.2 km and turn left at the "Forest Reserve" sign, onto TWP RD 4-3. Drive 5.5 km to the Victoria Ridge Trailhead. You may have to park outside the gates, about 50 m before the locked gate.

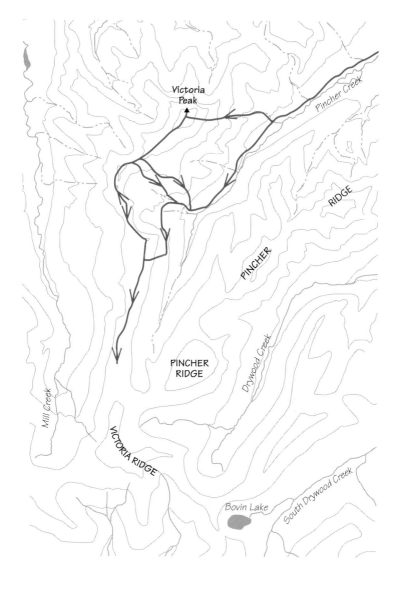

Victoria Peak

Pincher Creek

RIDGE

PINCHER

Drywood Creek

PINCHER
RIDGE

Mill Creek

VICTORIA RIDGE

Bovin Lake

South Drywood Creek

Hike or bike the road for approximately 3.5 km. Victoria Peak is the tallest and most shapely peak in the area and lies on the north side of the trail. Several ascent routes are possible, but the best one stays on the ridge immediately to the left of the major drainage that divides the mountain. Scramble easy slopes, picking up the odd trail here and there. Higher up you come across several bands of rock that can be tackled head-on or circumvented on the right. A line of trees to the right marks the route.

Once above the tree line, enjoy the wonderful variety of colourful rock as the terrain becomes steeper. Again, small rock bands can be ascended via weaknesses, or you can keep to the right to avoid them. A short section of moderate scrambling will lead you to the ridge only minutes away from the summit. Turn right and you're practically there.

The colourful summit panorama is quite impressive and includes Pincher Ridge to the southeast, Mount Gladstone to the northwest, and Prairie Bluffs to the northeast. Most notable, however, is the striking form of Castle Peak connected to Windsor Mountain to the west.

Return the same way, or, for an easier descent, trend left once below the rock band at the top. Find scree slopes that lead all the way down to the major drainage. Near the bottom, you may want to traverse to the right, through the trees and back to the original ascent route. This helps avoid some potentially annoying bushwhacking farther down.

For a scenic and more than worthwhile extension of the trip, head southwest from the summit and follow the long ridge—appropriately called Victoria Ridge. Initially, the ridge is undulating and jagged with a precipitous drop on the east side, but it soon flattens out. Throughout, the extension is mostly hiking with some easy scrambling and no exposure. See the Victoria Ridge description for the remainder of the details.

Victoria Ridge 2,530 m

Difficulty Easy; mostly hiking
Round-trip time 5–10 hours
Elevation gain 1,050 m
Maps 82 G/8 Beaver Mines; 82 G/1 Sage Creek

Victoria Ridge extends south from Victoria Peak, eventually forming a horseshoe with Pincher Ridge. The trip can be done in conjunction with an ascent of Victoria Peak or by itself. Either way, the spectacular scenery and colours put it in the "must do" category, even though the ascent would more accurately be described as a hike, not a scramble. Wait for a blue-sky day. Try from June on.

Linda Breton on the ridge connecting Victoria Peak to the summit of Victoria Ridge. VR summit of Victoria Ridge.

Park as for Victoria Peak at the Victoria Ridge trailhead. Hike or bike the gravel road for 4 km until it stops and becomes a trail. Leave your bike here and hike the pleasant trail through the valley. Eventually it curves right, heading uphill through the trees. Higher up, the trail goes left under the impressive walls of one of the many high points along the ridge and then goes south paralleling the ridge. At this point, it is best to turn right and ascend easy slopes to the ridge. This route is more scenic than remaining on the trail below the ridge, but it will require additional elevation losses and gains. Once on the ridge, turn left and head south toward the high point of the ridge some distance away. You will have to drop to a low col before making the final push to the summit of Victoria Ridge. Be sure to stop occasionally and enjoy the colourful views of Pincher Ridge. **Return** the same way, but follow the directions below to get the most out of the trip by traversing a portion of the ridge toward Victoria Peak.

If you don't feel like completing the long ridgewalk all the way to the summit of Victoria Ridge, gain the ridge as described above, and turn north instead of south. The first cairned high point is easily gained. Continue north along the jagged ridge that now has a precipitous drop on the right. A few small drop-offs can easily be circumvented by dropping down a short distance to the left. Upon reaching the next and most prominent high point, the ridge descends to a low col that separates Victoria Ridge from Victoria Peak. If you have the energy, it's a straightforward scree/rubble ascent to the summit of Victoria Peak from here. If not, pick one of several descent routes back to the trail (see photo below). If snow persists in the valley below you, one of the routes that stays high and avoids travel through the trees is recommended. The high road will also maximize your exposure to the terrific scenery.

Many choices for descent. C low col. VP summit of Victoria Peak. V valley. H the high descent route.

Pincher Ridge 2,423 m

Difficulty Difficult; sections of steep, exposed scrambling;
route-finding challenges
Round-trip time 6.5–8 hours
Elevation gain 900 m
Maps 82 G/8 Beaver Mines

When seen from Drywood Mountain, Pincher Ridge presents the beautifully rounded contour and spectacular colours of its south side. And like Drywood, there is also a more challenging ascent route, followed by a much easier descent route. The rock is loose, but the interesting scenery and amazing colours should be more than enough motivation to try this peak. Try from June on.

From Pincher Creek, head south toward Waterton. About 20.5 km south of the south end of Pincher Creek, take Highway 505 west (the east turnoff comes up first—don't take it!). Follow the 505 for 9.2 km and turn left at the "Forest

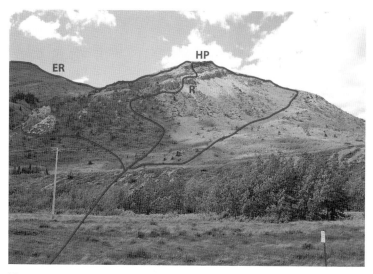

Three routes to the ridge. Middle route is the most scenic. R colourful rock bands. HP easterly high point of east ridge. ER east ridge.

Reserve" sign, onto TWP RD 4-3. Drive 3.9 km and turn left onto RGE RD 1-2A. Follow the road for 2.1 km and park to the right of the locked gate.

From the parking area, head northwest to gain the east ridge. There are many possible routes to the ridge, however, the most visually rewarding route intersects the prominent rock outcrop, lining the upper section of the ridge (see photo above). Once at the rock, be sure to explore the terrain a little, before cutting through the rock bands to gain the ridge. Either continue up to the most easterly high point of the ridge or trend left, side-sloping toward a point on the ridge farther west. On the ridge, head west toward a series of bands of rock that line the striking east ridge.

Eventually, you'll arrive at a vertical rock band that bars the way. Traverse along and down it on the left side. Once around, start side-sloping the scree (heading southwest), passing by one rib. It is possible to continue side-sloping and then gain the ridge closer to the summit, however, the most interesting route gains the ridge quickly. Look for a water-worn, grey-rock gully and ascend its step-like terrain to an obvious weakness (break) in the rock band to the left. Go up this rock band. It is steeper than it looks and involves a few difficult moves, but the rock is solid.

Gain the east ridge again and continue up until the next band rears up. A detailed description from here is unnecessary. Ascend the ridge circumventing

East ridge. G gully. S summit.

steeper sections on either side of the ridge (which side is usually obvious). Higher up, the right side is best.

About 40 vertical metres from the summit, detour onto the north side of the mountain and route-find your way up steep, grassy slopes toward the ridge. This may require a couple of short but necessary elevation losses, as well as several exposed moves up very steep terrain right before the ridge. Upon gaining the ridge, the summit is only a short distance away to the east.

The west ridge and southwest slopes offer an easy and stress-free **return** route. Follow the ridge west until you can trend left onto the light brown slopes of shale. Descend these gentle slopes, more or less directly to the gravel road far below. Expect a short stint of bush-bashing just before the road. It's a 4-km hike back to your vehicle once you reach the valley bottom.

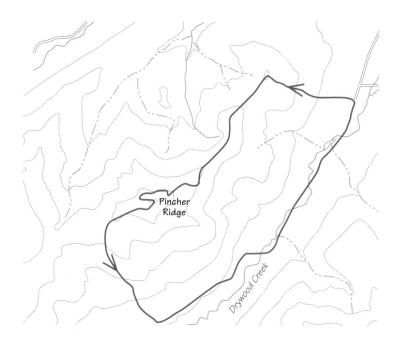

Drywood Mountain 2,514 m

Difficulty Moderate via south slopes
Round-trip time 7–10 hours for the loop
Elevation gain 840 m; 500 m loss and gain to west summit
Maps 82 G/8 Beaver Mines, 82 G/1 Sage Creek

Drywood Mountain offers the typical fare of amazing colours and interesting scenery, common to peaks in the area. The loop route features a more challenging ascent, with an easy and scenic descent, and is the recommended route. Fit parties can continue on to the summit of Loaf Mountain to the south. Try from mid-June on.

From Pincher Creek, head south toward Waterton. About 20.5 km south of the south end of Pincher Creek, take Highway 505 west (the east turnoff comes up first—don't take it!). Follow the 505 for 9.2 km and turn left at the "Forest Reserve" sign, onto TWP RD 4-3. Drive 3.9 km and turn left onto RGE RD 1-2A. Drive for 1.4 km and turn left onto TWP RD 4-2. Follow the road for 5.1 km and turn right. You'll find the Bovin Lake Trailhead sign about 200 m

Drywood Mountain, as seen from the east end of Loaf Mountain. CR crux rock band. S summit. LR loop route. FS false summit of west end.

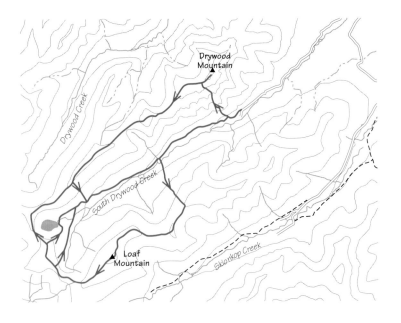

down the road. If the gate is open (June 15–September 1), drive 4 km to the final gas well and park near the road (trail) that veers off to the right.

Hike for several minutes along the Bovin Lake Trail, looking to your right for an obvious ascent line that has been cut through the mountain by water (see photo on p. 78). Turn right and make your way through light bush to the start of the drainage. Enjoy easy to moderate scrambling as you ascend the water-worn rock of the gully. The only major obstacle is a steep band of rock that lines the south face, going up to the right. Water may be pouring down this step when you reach it. There are two ways to get above the band. Either back down a little and look for a weakness on the left side of the watercourse or traverse up and along the base of the band until you arrive at another weakness. Ascending this step involves several exposed moves on steep rock. If not to your liking, return to the watercourse and ascend the left side.

Above the band, continue following the watercourse up more steppy terrain until you reach a band of burgundy argillite. Start trending left toward easier terrain marked by a black band. Ascend this band to the ridge and turn right. Follow the ridge easily to the summit

Either **return** the same way, or extend the day by choosing the longer, but easier, descent route along the west ridge. Start by heading back the way you came, but instead of cutting left onto the south-facing descent slopes, keep going straight in a westerly direction toward the slightly higher west summit. This traverse is long and involves approximately 500 m of elevation loss, which all must then be regained, yet the terrain is easy, scenic, and requires no route-finding. Expect to take 2–3 hours from the east summit to the west summit. At the west summit, continue heading west along the ridge toward Bovin Lake. When the lake becomes visible, turn left and head down easy slopes to hook up with the Bovin Lake Trail. Turn left onto the trail and hike the easy trail back to your vehicle.

If the summit of Loaf Mountain is also on the agenda for the day, stay on the ridge as it circles Bovin Lake and then swing around to tackle Loaf's west slopes—an easy but exceedingly long extension. Loaf Mountain's ascent route can then be used for the descent.

Loaf Mountain 2,640 m

Difficulty Easy via northwest slopes
Round-trip time 6–8 hours
Elevation gain 1,000 m
Maps 82 G/8 Beaver Mines, 82 G/1 Sage Creek

The most interesting route to the summit of this peak traverses the entire ridge starting from the east. Unfortunately, this route quickly becomes technical and requires rope work. The route described below is far easier, though somewhat more mundane. The height of the mountain and the views from the top make this

Loaf Mountain from the approach trail. FS false summit. (photo by Linda Breton)

The ascent drainage.

a worthwhile trip. Very fit and fast parties can ascend Drywood first, complete a very long loop route to the summit of Loaf, and then use the described route for descent. Save it for a clear day. Try from mid-June on.

Follow the driving directions for Drywood Mountain (on pp. 77 and 79). From the gate, drive 4 km to the final gas well. The road/trail that veers off to the right just before the gas well is the trail you'll be on. Unless your vehicle has monster-truck tires and 4 feet (1.2 m) of clearance, don't even think about trying to drive it.

Hike or bike the trail for several kilometres, keeping your eye on the "loaf" shaped mass on the left (see photo on p. 80). Coincidentally, this is a false summit, that, like the true summit, resembles a rising loaf of bread. You'll be ascending easy slopes to the east of this mass. Look for a good place to cross the creek and gain these slopes without too much bushwhacking (see photo). There is a good drainage that you'll want to aim for.

The slopes are tedious, but at least the drainage offers a little visual interest and the feeling that you are actually scrambling, if only in a minor way. Once you gain the ridge, if you have time, turn left and follow the beautiful and very wide red argillite ridge to a high point that overlooks the east end of the mountain. This diversion is simply for the view. If that doesn't interest you, turn right upon gaining the ridge and follow it up and over the false summit and then easily onto the true summit.

Second in elevation only to Mount Glendowan in the general area, Loaf provides a splendid viewpoint. To the south lies lengthy Spionkop Ridge, with the equally interesting Drywood Mountain immediately to the north. Most eye-catching, however, is the snake-like contour of Loaf to the east.

Returning the same way is fast and easy. A more interesting and longer, but still very easy, descent is to continue down the gentle southwest slopes. At the bottom, curve around to the northwest and either find the trail (easily visible from above) that joins up with the Bovin Lake Trail via forested terrain, or continue northwest up to the next high point for a good aerial view of Bovin Lake. Traverse the ridge and then drop down to the lake through light forest. At the lake, walk around to the northeast side, where you'll find the Bovin Lake Trail. It's 6.4 km back to your car from there.

It is also possible to stay on the ridge, circle Bovin Lake from above and head northeast to the two summits of Drywood Mountain. This option, however, is far more enjoyable when done in reverse.

Another extension for the day is to descend the southwest slopes and then continue south to the summit of Spionkop Ridge (2,576 m). You can then avoid too much unnecessary elevation gain on return by using the alternate descent route described above.

Mount Roche 2,492 m

Difficulty Moderate with one difficult step via northeast ridge
Round-trip time 7–10 hours
Elevation gain 1,000 m
Maps 82 G/1 Sage Creek

Mount Roche (locally named Spread Eagle Mountain) is a prominent high point at the east end of 7-km long Spionkop Ridge. The scrambling is generally excellent and interesting throughout, though much of the rock is covered in lichen and is very slippery when wet. Wait for a dry day to best enjoy the scrambling and a clear day to best enjoy the colourful scenery and views. Try from July on.

Both ascent and descent routes from the gas road. S summit. D descent route.

From the south end of Pincher Creek, drive 31.2 km south on Highway 6 and turn right onto TWP 3-4 (4.3 km south of the General Store in Twin Butte). Drive 8 km to the end of the road. Turn right onto Yarrow Road and drive 4 km to a bridge that crosses Spionkop Creek. Park at the hairpin turn immediately after the bridge. The trail starts here, heading west between Loaf Mountain to the north and Roche to the south. Hike the trail, eventually crossing to the south side of the creek. Continue west for a while, ignoring the multitude of animal trails heading south. Soon the trail does turn south and up. Follow it through light forest until the terrain opens up with a rocky hill to your right. Either ascend the hill right away or traverse the east side of it for a few hundred metres and then pick a line of ascent. This will put you at the far east end of Spionkop Ridge (Mount Roche).

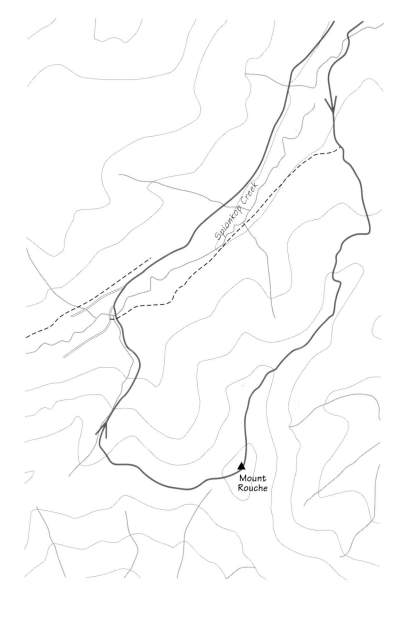

Splonkop Creek

Mount
Rouche

Follow the ridge west, up and over a couple of bumps to the start of the scrambling. When it does start, the best (and steepest) scrambling is found on the edge of the ridge. Go right for easier terrain. A steeper rock band soon comes up and can be ascended via one of several weaknesses. Traverse alongside the band to find one to your liking. Your best bet may be the second gully from the south end. If this band gives you problems, you may want to consider an alternative objective, as the crux will prove to be more difficult and exposed than the band itself.

Continue up the ridge to arrive at the crux—a high, vertical band of rock that is a staple of many of the surrounding mountains (Loaf, Drywood, Dungarvan, Glendowan, etc.). Head north, losing elevation alongside the band for several hundred metres to find the weakness. It is characterized by a small but noticeable example of rock folding, seen when you scramble up to the base. This crux step only involves a couple of tricky moves but is steep and exposed. Descending this step would likely require a rope. Fortunately, an alternate descent route eliminates that need—provided you make it to the top!

Regain the ridge and continue on to the summit. Choose your own line from here. The fastest, but least interesting ascent, takes a line that side-slopes and stays well right of the ridge on easier terrain. Stay on the ridge as much as possible to maximize your scrambling experience. The summit view features mountains of Waterton to the south and southwest and other familiar peaks of the Castle to the north and northwest. This is a good vantage point to see the entire length of Loaf Mountain and scope out potential routes from the south side, though the ascent route described in this book goes up the north side of the peak. The lower connecting peak a few hundred metres to the southeast is another unofficial peak called Mount Yarrow and can be reached easily from the summit of Roche.

Either **return** the same way—provided you can downclimb or rappel the crux—or for a much easier escape off the mountain, start heading west. Drop down to a col and then up to the next minor high point, where the descent route is visible to the northwest—a hanging valley with a drainage in the middle. Descend easy slopes in a northwest direction, alongside a small forest of larches on the way to the drainage. There is an animal trail on the other side of the drainage, but eventually you'll want to be on the side you're already on (the right side of the drainage). Follow the drainage out (now heading northeast), staying above the trees and vegetation. The drainage soon drops off, but you can traverse under the growing rock bands on the right to scree slopes that go all the way down to another drainage. Follow that drainage out to the trail or the easier gas well road. A 4-km walk takes you back to your vehicle.

West Castle

Mount Gladstone	2,458 m	moderate	page 86
Table Mountain	2,225 m	easy	page 89
Syncline Mountain	2,500 m	easy/moderate	page 92
St. Eloi Mountain	2,500 m	easy	page 95
Mount Haig	2,618 m	moderate	page 97
Gravenstafel Ridge	2,394 m	easy	page 100

Perhaps the most intriguing characteristic of the West Castle area is the uniqueness of each mountain: from the colourful high plateau of aptly named Table Mountain, to the pleasant ridgewalk of St. Eloi, to the impressive northeast face of Mount Haig. My personal favourite is Syncline Mountain, which offers a long but thoroughly entertaining traverse of its three summits.

These peaks are accessed from Highways 507 and 774, west of Pincher Creek.

The enjoyable traverse from the second summit of Syncline Mountain to the third summit.

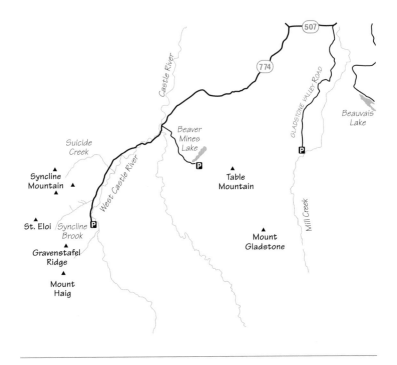

Mount Gladstone 2,458 m

Difficulty Moderate via southeast slopes
Round-trip time 5–8 hours
Elevation gain 1,000 m
Maps 82 G/8 Beaver Mines

The scrambling on Mount Gladstone is minimal, but the mountain does offer interesting scenery, varied terrain, a fine summit panorama, and a terrific alternate descent route. Save the trip for a clear, autumn day. Try from June on.

Drive to Pincher Creek and turn right onto Highway 507 west. Drive 15.5 km and turn left onto Gladstone Valley Road. Follow the gravel road for 13.9 km and turn right at an unmarked intersection, 0.6 km after the second bridge. Drive another 3.2 km along this road, staying right when it forks to a gas well site and a small grassy parking area by the ATV trail signs.

Hike 100 m alongside a barbed wire fence to a small grassy clearing. Find a wide trail that curves left, continues for 50 m, and then becomes a horse trail as it turns right and heads into the forest. This trail is a little more circuitous than the ATV trail, but it is easy, straightforward, and means you'll only have to cross Mill Creek once. Hike this trail for about 35 minutes (it eventually merges with the ATV trail) until you arrive at Mill Creek (GR038676). Across the creek, a distinctive, unnamed outlier will be to your left and the east slopes of Gladstone to your right. You will be heading right in between them.

Cross Mill Creek—it may be flowing, it may be dry, it may be low, it may be high. (Watch out Shakespeare!) Find the trail on the other side. Cross another dried-up creek bed and follow the trail back into the trees as it starts to head up and alongside the slopes of Gladstone. Soon the trail takes a sharp right and starts to traverse Gladstone's east slopes. From the crossing of Mill Creek, hike the trail for about 50 minutes to one of several rocky drainages (see photo). The entire ascent route is visible from here.

Ascend the drainage, either right up the middle or on the right side. The ascent is mostly steep hiking, but the interesting rock is enough to entertain. Higher up, two significant bands of black rock are visible to the left. The top

The ascent route from the trail. S summit.

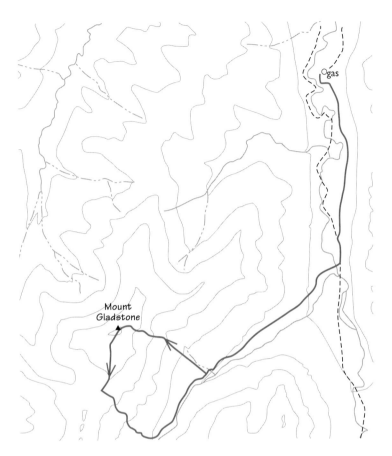

of the first is easily gained by traversing left before it starts to become significant. Continue up alongside the second black band (the last obstacle before the summit) until you reach the ridge. Then back down a few metres to find an obvious weakness in the band. The last few metres takes you up a grove of smoother rock that is steeper, but there are good holds. Once at the top of this, the summit is only a few metres away.

Undoubtedly, the splendid view of striking Castle Peak and its partner Windsor Mountain to the right will garner most of your attention. Table and Whistler Mountains are immediately north, with the familiar peaks of the Crowsnest beyond. The tall peak to the southeast is Victoria Peak and Victoria Ridge heading west from the peak—two excellent trips themselves.

The alternate **return** route is a must do. Continue southwest along the ridge and then down rubble, grass, and scree slopes to a low col, characterized by red argillite scree. Turn southeast down the argillite slopes. Scree surfing this slope is not only super fast and fun but a colourful visual reward, as well. When the red argillite runs out, traverse left onto light brown scree and continue down, paralleling the drainage. Near the bottom, cross onto the right side of the drainage and continue down along the left side of thick foliage. Arrive shortly at the trail, turn left, and it's an easy hike back to the parking area.

Table Mountain 2,225 m

Difficulty Easy via southwest slopes
Round-trip time 3.5–5 hours
Elevation gain 740 m
Maps 82 G/8 Beaver Mines

A great choice if time and/or energy are limited. Table Mountain has a very short approach, interesting scenery, varied terrain, and won't leave you searching on e-Bay afterwards for a new set of lungs. Yet again, doing the ascent in autumn rewards you with the beautiful yellows of changing larches. Try from June on.

Drive to Pincher Creek and turn right onto Highway 507, following signs for Castle Mountain Ski Resort. At the T-intersection, turn left, heading southwest on 774, and drive 15 km to the Beaver Mines Lake turnoff. Turn left onto the

Table Mountain, seen from highway 774. S summit. WP western plateau.

road and go 5.5 km, arriving at a pull-off on the right side, near the Table Mountain trailhead sign.

Hike the Table Mountain Trail for about 20 minutes. At the second big clearing, leave the trail and head up slopes on your left (see photo below). The ascent route goes up between the two outliers visible ahead. Either go straight up toward the western outlier (left) or traverse right to find a trail that makes life a little easier. Either way, you will eventually have to work your way to the right in order to find a weakness on the left side of the gully that grants easy access to the upper slopes. Ascend this weakness. Once above the weakness, either continue straight up the middle of the upper slopes or trend left to gain the west ridge. Both routes join up later as you head to the left side of the interesting summit block of the western plateau (not the true summit).

Though this block may appear intimidating from afar, there is a weakness at the far left. It is possible to bypass the block altogether by heading to its right side, however, the layers of beautifully coloured rock are definitely worth a

The ascent route from the trail.

close-up look. At the top of the western plateau, the rest of the route is obvious, easy, and not as far as it looks. On the way, you pass through a small larch tree forest (very pleasant in late September, when they are changing colour). The summit view is decent, though perhaps a little anticlimactic after the interesting ascent.

Return the same way. It is not necessary to go all the way back to the western plateau. Once back at the col, simply side-slope scree on the left side of the plateau, back to the ascent slopes. Everything is the same after that.

Upper slopes. G gully. WP western Plateau.

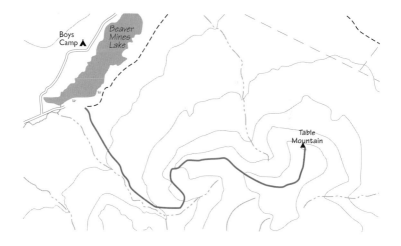

Syncline Mountain 2,500 m

Difficulty Easy to first summit; moderate to second; difficult
(but avoidable) scrambling to the third
Round-trip time 3.5–5 hours to first summit; 9–12 hours for
all 3 summits
Elevation gain 1,020 m to first summit; add approx. 400 m for
second and third summits
Maps 82 G/8 Beaver Mines

*Syncline Mountain sports three separate summits. Inexplicably, the lowest of the
three is actually the true summit. This one can be easily reached from the road in
short order. The best part of the trip, however, belongs to ascents of the second and
third (highest) peaks. The rock scenery along the way is absolutely wonderful. Try
from July on.*

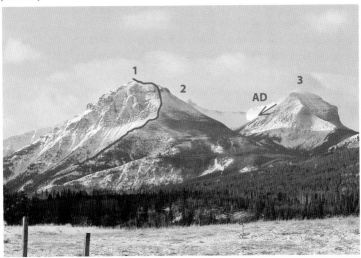

The three summits of Syncline from Highway 774. AD alternate descent route.

Drive to Pincher Creek and turn right onto Highway 507, following the signs
for Castle Mountain Ski Resort. At the T-intersection, turn left and head southwest on 774, then park on the side of the road 23.5 km south of the intersection (GR881700). The entire route to the first summit is visible from the road.

Head west through light forest aiming for the northeast ridge. Once on
more open slopes, trend a little left and ascend the left side of the slopes all the
way to the summit ridge—this will at least give you some decent views along

The route to the second summit from the first summit. HP worthwhile high point to visit. T traverse around the high point.

the way. Gain the summit ridge through an obvious weakness between two outcrops of rock, turn left and walk to the summit cairn, a couple of minutes away. Technically, you have now reached the true summit of the mountain. It is, however, not the highest one, and certainly not the most interesting of the three. If content, **return** the same way.

The two higher summits of Syncline can be seen to the southwest and northwest of the first summit. The most interesting route follows the ridge for some sections and traverses below it for others. Continue south along the ridge and drop down to a col (don't be tempted to take a more direct route down to the valley to the west.) Gaining the high point in front of you is a worthwhile diversion, requiring minimal effort, but you will have to return to the col. Once back at the col, descend slopes to the right and traverse along the base of the huge rock outcrop. This takes you to another col and another rock outcrop.

From here, it is possible to pick your way down the right side of the mountain to the low col that separates the two summits. A more scenic (but longer) option goes around the other side and is described here. Both options require a significant elevation loss. Go around to the left (south) side of the ridge and

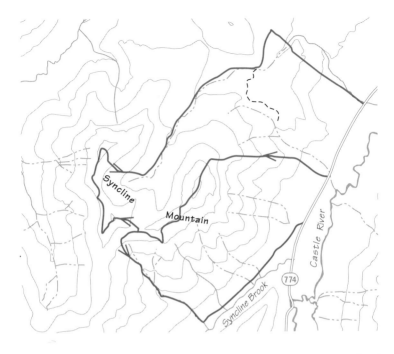

traverse below it until you arrive at a severe drop-off. You now have to head down scree slopes to your left until a feasible route around the cliffs presents itself. Once low enough, traverse along the base of the impressive and colourful cliffs back to the ridge, staying high on the slopes. A scree slog then leads easily to the second summit.

The view from the second summit is splendid, especially south toward Eloi, Gravenstafel, and Haig. Farther southwest, Tombstone Mountain is easily recognizable because of its shape. The best view is looking back to the first summit and the scenic ridge you've negotiated to get to the second.

Yet again, you now have the option to call it a day or continue on to the third and highest summit. To **return**, go back down to the low col and then south, down scree slopes into the drainage that eventually leads to Syncline Brook Trail. Turn left onto the trail and follow it back to the road. Your vehicle will be about 1 km north.

The trickiest part of the traverse to the third summit comes right at the beginning. Don't head north along the ridge—you'll get cliffed-out within minutes. Instead, scramble down to the southwest, looking for a steepish scree gully, which gets you below the steep layers of rock that surround you. When onto easier terrain, turn north and traverse scree slopes to the connecting ridge. Follow the ridge to the summit. Two rock bands rear up just before the top. Both are easily circumvented by going onto scree slopes to the right. It's far more enjoyable, however, to tackle them head-on. Both involve steep, exposed scrambling and the rock must be dry.

The first rock band is initially overhanging. Traverse to the right a few metres and a steep crack becomes visible. Ascend it making one or two awkward moves over a chockstone and then continue up another steep band of brown rock. The second, a lichen-covered black rock band, is a little more serious. Once you start up, you won't want to go back down, so be sure of your route. At the top, the summit is only minutes away.

Getting back to your vehicle from the third summit maybe the crux of your day. There are several options. You could **return** the same way (recommended only for those with Herculean endurance!). You could also **return** to the second summit and use the descent route described above or, from the summit, descend southeast facing slopes into the valley below. Follow the creek out (Suicide Creek). Be prepared for sections of downright nasty bushwhacking. Much lower down, ATV trails appear on the left side of the creek. If you're lucky, you'll find one right away. If not, stay near the creek as much as possible and eventually you will run into a trail. Turn right and follow ATV and hiking trails back to the road, coming out of the forest about 1.3 km north of your vehicle.

St. Eloi Mountain 2,500 m

Difficulty Easy via northeast ridge
Round-trip time 5.5–7 hours
Elevation gain 1,100 m
Maps 82 G/8 Beaver Mines

In between the more challenging scrambles of Syncline and Haig sits St. Eloi Mountain. It is long enough and scenic enough to be considered a separate trip. Only very fast and very fit parties will want to consider continuing north to Syncline or south to Haig. Try from June on.

Drive to Pincher Creek and turn right onto Highway 507, following signs for Castle Mountain Ski Resort. At the T-intersection, turn left, heading southwest on 774, and park on the side of the road approximately 24.5 km south of the intersection, at the Syncline Brook Trailhead.

Hike the trail for approximately 1.5 km (20–30 minutes), arriving at a large, rocky drainage with flagging on either side. Turn right and hike up the

The ascent drainage. D drainage. R ridge. SS Syncline's second summit.

Route from the ridge. HP subsidiary high point. S summit of Eloi.

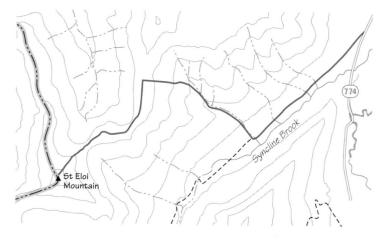

drainage for a fair distance, looking for open slopes on the left that lead to the ridge that connects Eloi (left) to Syncline (right). Ascend the foreshortened slopes to the ridge and turn left toward Eloi. Follow the ridge to the summit. Though an intervening high point can be side-sloped on the left side, gaining the high point requires minimal effort and is worth a quick visit.

Shapely Mount Haig dominates to the south and appropriately named Tombstone Mountain farther west. To the north, the three summits of Syncline are particularly pleasing to the eye. **Return** the same way.

Mount Haig 2,618 m

Difficulty Moderate via northeast and east ridges
Round-trip time 6–8 hours; add 1–2 hours for Gravenstafel Ridge
Elevation gain 1,100 m; add 300 m for Gravenstafel Ridge
Maps 82 G/8 Beaver Mines

Mount Haig is the highest mountain in the general area and a worthwhile scramble. Continuing north to the summit of Gravenstafel Ridge gives you two official summits for the day and is part of an excellent loop route.

Drive to Pincher Creek and turn right onto Highway 507, following signs for Castle Mountain Ski Resort. At the T-intersection, turn left, heading southwest on 774, and park at the Castle Mountain Ski Resort.

To the southwest lies the northeast ridge of Haig, now home to a new ski lift. Make your way over to the ski lift and follow it up to its terminus. Con-

Route to the east ridge, from the northeast ridge.

The alternate descent route(s), seen from the summit of Haig. C Haig/Gravenstafel col. L route to the lake. G summit of Gravenstafel Ridge. S Syncline. E St. Eloi.

tinue up the northeast ridge to its high point. Here, you'll be privy to a great view of Haig's awesome northeast face, the east ridge route (that you'll shortly be on), the alternate loop descent route, and the extension to Gravenstafel Ridge.

Now comes the tough part—a necessary elevation loss down to the lake (pond) in between the northeast and east ridges. Once down, ascend easy slopes to the east ridge. Follow the ridge to the summit. There are a few opportunities to enjoy some hands-on scrambling up minor rock bands, so take advantage of them. For easier terrain, traverse left alongside the bands, until you find a weakness to your liking. Most notably, the summit view includes mountains in the Waterton southeast, Castle east, and Crowsnest north and northwest.

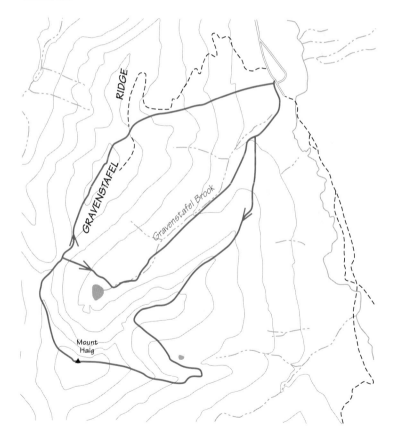

St. Eloi and Syncline, two other worthwhile scrambles, sit immediately to the north.

Either **return** the same way, or do the loop route, which is easier, interesting, and therefore recommended. Continue down the north ridge, keeping the col between Haig and Gravenstafel Ridge in mind—that's where you're heading. As you approach the first low point on the ridge, look to the right for an obvious trail that starts heading down to the col. The following section is the only one of consequence as the terrain gets steeper and there is even a touch of exposure! The route down is well marked by the trail and shouldn't pose any problems.

Gravenstafel Ridge 2,394 m

If you've had enough, make your way down to the small lake nestled under the northeast face of Haig, find the trail at the lake's east side, and follow it back to the parking area. If you're up for an easy additional 300 m of elevation gain and another summit under your belt, continue north up the south ridge of Gravenstafel Ridge. Stay on the ridge and tackle all bands head-on. One rock band, about halfway up, is a little more challenging, but there are weaknesses and easier routes on both sides. A few false summits later and you're up (40–50 minutes from the col).

Getting down is easy. Continue north along the ridge for a few minutes until a maze of ski runs and maintenance roads become visible. Choose whatever line you like to the bottom. The maintenance roads are circuitous but less steep, however, going straight down is never difficult either.

South Kananaskis

Kananaskis Country extends from the Trans-Canada Highway in the north to Highway 532 about 100 km south, encompassing an area of approximately 4,000 square kilometres. While there is no official distinction between "South" and "North" Kananaskis, dividing the area into two sections seems appropriate for the purposes of this guidebook. Since Highway 40 is closed between the Kananaskis Road turnoff and Highwood Junction from December 1 to June 15, I've designated the Kananaskis turnoff as the starting point of South Kananaskis. All peaks south of that point are included in this section. Be aware that the road closure on Highway 40 renders many of these peaks inaccessible during that period of time.

Many of the routes in this section, specifically those on the Continental Divide, are a great distance from the highway and require lengthy approaches. Fortunately for scramblers and hikers (but unfortunately for the environment) old logging roads allow you to bike many of the approaches. That is not to say that you are going to be covering 10 km in 45 minutes of super-speed bike riding. Many of the trails are rough when dry and a muddy mess when wet. In addition, streams frequently cross these trails, further slowing you down. Attempting to negotiate these trails too early in the season may mean you are pushing your bike through muddy puddles more than riding it. Nevertheless, the reward of making it to the Continental Divide is clearly evident in the wild and breath-taking surroundings (see pp. 16–18 for more information on biking the approaches and river crossings).

This entire area is thoroughly documented and described in Gillean Daffern's *Kananaskis Country Trail Guide, Volume 2*. This outstanding resource gives detailed descriptions to many of the approaches to scrambles in this section and should be on your bookshelf or in your backpack.

Geology

Kananaskis is all about limestone, and lots of it! The quality of the rock ranges from amazing to downright atrocious. Unfortunately, much of the limestone in South Kananaskis fits into the latter category, especially the piles of rubble along the Continental Divide. Of course, there are exceptions to this rule, and certainly there are sections of enjoyable scrambling on solid rock throughout the area—just be prepared to hike a long way to get to them.

In contrast to the horizontally laid beds of the Waterton and Castle areas, the orientation of the rock in Kananaskis is more vertical. This is the result of two crustal plates colliding millions of years ago, pushing the rock upward and at the same time bending and folding it. Many of the peaks in the area display the classic northwest to southeast alignment that resulted from the collision. Mount Rundle, in Banff National Park, offers an obvious example, with its steep, northeast face contrasting nicely with the more gently graded slopes on the southwest side of the peak.

Climate and Weather

Since this section contains mountains in the front ranges and those farther west along the Continental Divide, the climate varies a fair amount. Typically, the front range peaks receive less precipitation and therefore enjoy a longer scrambling season. Once the Continental Divide peaks receive snow, usually in November, it is unlikely they will clear off until the following summer. That's okay … you can't get to them anyway because of the road closure!

Access

Most of the peaks in this section lie off the south section of Highway 40. That road can be reached via the Trans-Canada from the north, or via Highway 22 at Longview from the south. In general, from Calgary, the drive via Longview is shorter. From Calgary, drive south on Highway 2, taking the turnoff to Okotoks. Continue through the town of Okotoks and turn right (west) onto Highway 7. Follow it to Black Diamond and turn left (south) onto Highway 22. At Longview, turn right (west) onto Highway 541, which eventually turns into Highway 40 at the 940/40 junction.

Accommodation

If you plan on spending the night in South Kananaskis, you are basically relegated to one of several campgrounds along Highway 40 or motels and camping in Longview or Black Diamond.

Sheep River Area

East Peak of Mount Burns	2,622 m	moderate	page 104
Shunga-la-she	2,625 m	difficult	page 108
Junction Mountain	2,682 m	moderate	page 111

Looking east to the Sheep River area from the summit of Gibraltar Mountain.

Mount Burns

East Peak of Burns

▲ GR 565088

Sheep River

P

546

Gibraltar Mountain

Shunga-la-she

Junction Creek

Junction Mountain

The three peaks in the Sheep River area are all accessed from the Bluerock/Junction Creek Parking area, at the far end of Highway 546. To get there from Calgary, drive south on Highway 2, taking the turnoff to Okotoks (2A). Continue through the town of Okotoks and turn right (west) onto Highway 7. Follow it through Black Diamond, reaching Turner Valley 3 km after that. At the west side of Turner Valley, the road becomes Highway 546. The level of the Sheep River may dictate whether Junction and Shunga-la-she are feasible or not.

East Peak of Mount Burns at GR555096 2,622m

Difficulty Moderate with a few difficult sections via east ridge, some exposure
Round trip time 6–11 hours
Elevation gain 1,000 m
Maps 82 J/10 Mount Rae, Gem Trek Highwood & Cataract Creek

GR555096 is just one of the many high points of a long and interesting ridge that culminates with Mount Burns at 2,936 m. Though GR555096 is considerably lower, the ascent, while not terribly aesthetic, is interesting and not very long. A good objective for days when time and ambition may be lacking. For those with good downclimbing skills, a visit to GR565088 is a very pleasant diversion along the way. Try from June on.

Beginning of east ridge, seen from Sheep River Trail. H high ridge traverse. L low ridge traverse.

1 high point at GR570084. L traverse around left side. R traverse around right side. C crux. S summit of GR565088.

Drive to Turner Valley via Highway 7 west and continue through the hamlet, where the road soon turns into Highway 546. Drive to the end of the road and park at the lower section of the Bluerock/Junction Creek parking lot, close to the Sheep River. Hike the wide Sheep River Trail (starts from the upper section of the parking lot) for about 10 minutes. The objective is on your right and your goal is to quickly gain the east ridge (treed slopes rising from right to left). Turn right into the bush and head directly to the ridge through light forest. Once you're on the ridge, simply follow it upward. Above tree line, minor rock bands can be easily circumvented on the right side or tackled head-on. To get the most out of the scenery and views, return to the ridge edge as much as possible. At some points, it is actually more enjoyable to traverse along the bottom of the huge cliff bands (left side of the ridge) of the upper ridge. When it becomes obvious to do so, return to the ridge and continue to the first cairn at GR570084.

After reaching the first cairned high point, continue heading west on the ridge toward a rather daunting-looking summit block (GR565088). Upon reaching the base of the block, traverse around the right side for about 40 m, looking for a weakness to gain the first ledge. Scramble up and left to the wide ledge. There are two routes from here to the west side of the block.

Your first option is to head around the **right** side of the band. Quickly, it becomes easy to scramble up the rock band, trending left as you gain elevation. Just before the summit of GR565088, a steeper rock band rears up, guarding the summit. If you want to make a quick visit to the top, there is a weakness up and along a narrow ledge. Getting up the step is easy—getting down it is very difficult as there are no decent handholds and the terrain is exposed. A slip while descending the band would certainly result in a very serious fall. This downclimb is only for those who are extremely confident in their abilities. Most will want a good length of rope to set up an anchor and rappel down. If the summit of GR565088 is not on the agenda, keep traversing around the right side of the band, below the upper rock band. Quickly, you'll arrive at the west side of the block. This route is much shorter than its counterpart around the left side.

The crux of GR565088.

The second way to reach the west side of the block is to traverse **left** along the ledge around the entire band, regaining lost elevation when it is feasible. Stay high, close to the summit block. Regain the ridge at the west side of the block and continue heading west.

Stay on the ridge, circumventing the odd pinnacle on the left side. The ridge soon narrows as the terrain changes from crumbly shale to more solid limestone. A few mildly exposed moves on the right side of the ridge lead to a steeper rock band that can be ascended head-on or circumvented on grassy ledges on the right side. Atop this rock band, the remainder of the route is

The remainder of the route from the west side of GR565088. E easy route. D difficult route. S summit.

visible. Continue along the ridge. When steep rock bands bar the way, traverse right onto scree slopes that lead easily to the summit.

When finished admiring the very respectable summit view, which features a head-on view of the impressive 800-m vertical face of Gibraltar Mountain's north side, **return** the same way. Though it is tempting to escape to the Sheep River Trail directly from the summit via the south slopes, cliff bands and drop-offs abound and route-finding is challenging; this route is therefore not recommended.

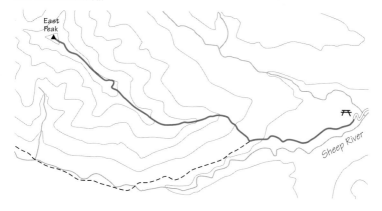

Shunga-la-she **2,625 m**

Difficulty Moderate with a few difficult sections via northeast ridge,
   some exposure
Round-trip time 6–9 hours
Elevation gain 1,000 m
Maps 82 J/10 Mount Rae, Gem Trek Highwood & Cataract Creek

*Oddly named Shunga-la-she has a good scramble route via its northeast ridge,
with options to extend the trip to a higher unnamed high point. As a front range
mountain, it is a good candidate for an early- or late-season trip, although there is
no access to the parking lot via Highway 546 from December 1 to May 15, and the
level of the Sheep River can be too high in the early season. Try from mid-June on.*

The route up the northeast ridge, from the Sheep River Trail. FS false summit

Drive to Turner Valley via Highway 7 west and continue through the hamlet,
where the road soon turns into Highway 546. Drive to the end of the road and
park on the lower section of the Bluerock/Junction Creek parking lot, close to
the Sheep River. Head west on the trail paralleling the Sheep River for a few
minutes and look for a decent place to cross the river. Descend steep slopes to
the river and cross. Hip-waders or runners would work well here, but if you
leave them on the other side of the river and then use the alternate descent
route, you'll have to cross again to retrieve them.

The alternate descent route down the north ridge.

Keep heading west. A pleasant jaunt through thin forest leads to the northeast ridge. GPS or a compass reading could save some unnecessary routefinding (or getting lost!). Eventually, the terrain starts going up and the forest gives way to a scree slope below a significant rock band. Unless you brought your rock shoes, circumvent the rock band easily on the left side and continue up the ridge. The remainder of the route is actually very straightforward from this point, however, numerous rock bands straddling the ridge complicate things a bit. Depending on your skill and comfort level, many of the bands can be tackled head-on—use good judgment and common sense. Others simply have to be circumvented, usually on the left side. Depending on how far you traverse alongside these bands, you may lose some elevation and then have to gain it back on labouriously steep scree slopes.

After gaining a couple of high points, it may be discouraging to discover that the summit is still some distance and elevation away. Persevere—the interesting rock scenery and great views of Gibraltar Mountain's daunting north face should be enough to keep your feet moving. Just before the summit, the ridge narrows considerably. This may or may not be the crux (depending on the route you've taken). Regardless, use caution as a slip here would probably be fatal. The summit is a minute beyond this step.

Enjoy a very respectable summit panorama, featuring the east faces of Mist, Storm, and Rae to the west, as well as Bluerock and Burns to the north. Junction, Pyriform, and many unnamed peaks of the Highwood Range dot the horizon to the south.

Return the same way, or take a far easier descent line down the west and northwest ridge. Continue heading west as the ridge curves down and then to the northwest. The goal is to descend into the obvious drainage to your left. Stay on the ridge until you see the easiest line down to the drainage. Once there, follow the drainage all the way down to the Sheep River Trail, which leads effortlessly back to the parking lot (don't forget to retrieve your hipwaders or runners if you left them on the other side of the Sheep River).

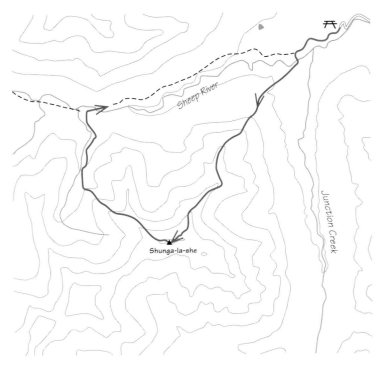

Junction Mountain 2,682 m

Difficulty Moderate with one difficult, exposed step via north ridge
Round-trip time 8–10 hours
Elevation gain 1,100 m
Maps 82 J/10 Mount Rae, Gem Trek Highwood & Cataract Creek

This trip involves a great deal of hiking with a few minor sections of interesting scrambling. The scenery is pleasant throughout, and the trip's considerable length should not deter those looking for an infrequently ascended peak. Try from mid-June on.

Drive to Turner Valley via Highway 7 west and continue through the hamlet, where the road soon turns into Highway 546. Drive to the end of the road and park on the lower section of the Bluerock/Junction Creek parking lot, close to the Sheep River. Go down to the river and ford it. Head southeast for a few minutes to arrive at Junction Creek—ford it as well. Continue in a southeast direction up steep, forested slopes to the first of many high points of the day.

Once on the ridge the route is obvious, but long. Hike along the ridge (south, southeast), over open and lightly forested slopes. Farther along, the ridge sometimes abruptly ends in minor drop-offs—downclimb them or back up a little and find an easier way around.

Several hours later, the ridge is interrupted by the prominent rock band—

The north ridge from the first high point. C crux. S summit.

the crux. Go around to the left side of the band, ascending slightly downsloping scree ledges, with an increasing drop-off to your left. After several hundred metres, you turn a corner where the scree ledge narrows and the exposure increases. Here you'll want to look to the right for a good place to ascend to the ridge. Backing up a little offers several options, but all require a few moves of difficult and exposed scrambling—pick your line carefully in case you have to downclimb to find an easier option.

The crux rock band. C crux.

On the ridge, turn left and enjoy sections of hiking and easy to moderate scrambling all the way to the summit. As is commonly the case, the ridge is best enjoyed by remaining on it, instead of on the faint trail below the right side of the ridge. Some sections, however, will have to be circumvented on the right. The ridge soon curves around to the right and descends to a col, where a short hike leads to the summit. The summit view takes in many of the beautiful but unnamed peaks of the Highwood Range. Pyriform and Mount Head lie to the south. The Elk Range can be seen to the west and Mount Harrison beyond that to the southwest.

Return the same way. If you want to avoid the crux, return to the small col below the summit and descend north-facing scree slopes. Side-slope until you can regain the ridge north of the crux rock band.

An alternate descent exists via Junction Creek. Route-finding can be tricky

Alternate descent route to the southwest.

so have a good map with you. This route allows you to visit the beautiful three-tiered waterfall near Junction Creek, but it is circuitous and will likely take at least 4 hours. From the top, descend tedious rubble and scree in the middle of the slope, aiming for the meadows to the southwest. Hike down through the meadows, staying well to the left. If you're lucky, you'll find a trail that trends southwest and then turns northwest to eventually intersect Junction Creek. If not, go in those directions anyway!

At Junction Creek, turn north and follow the creek if you haven't found a good trail. Eventually, waterfalls prevent you from staying near the creek. Ascend slopes on the left (west) side of the creek and continue north. Soon you should find a well-used trail that parallels the creek high above it. When this trail intersects a side creek coming from the west, cross it and turn left for a quick visit to the waterfalls, which are well worth a 10-minute detour. Return to the Junction Creek Trail and follow it back to the parking lot.

River

Sheep

Mount
Hoffman

Junction Creek

Junction
Mountain

Cataract Creek and Highwood

Holy Cross Mountain	2,685 m	easy/moderate	page 117
Mount Head	2,782 m	moderate/difficult	page 119
"Lineham Creek Peaks"	2,716 m	moderate/difficult	page 124
Lineham Ridge and GR593982	2,807 m	moderate	page 128
Gibraltar Mountain	2,665 m	moderate	page 131
Mount Odlum	2,716 m	moderate	page 134
Mount Loomis	2,822 m	moderate/difficult	page 136
Mount Bishop	2,850 m	moderate	page 140
Mount McPhail	2,865 m	easy/moderate	page 142
Mount Muir	2,743 m	easy	page 145
Mount Strachan	2,682 m	easy	page 146
Mount Armstrong	2,804 m	moderate	page 150

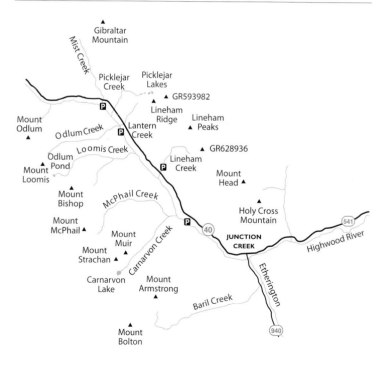

These peaks lie in the southern section of Kananaskis Country, off Highway 40 (identified as Highway 541, east of the 940/40 junction at Highwood Junction). Again, the driving approach from the south via Longview is probably quicker than the one via the Trans-Canada from the north. From Calgary, drive south on Highway 2, taking the turnoff to Okotoks (2A). Continue through the town of Okotoks and turn right (west) onto Highway 7. Follow it to Black Diamond and turn left (south) onto Highway 22. At Longview turn right (west) onto Highway 541.

Only Holy Cross Mountain, Mount Head, Mount Armstrong, and Mount Bolten can be accessed year-round. Access to the other scrambles is restricted due to the closure of Highway 40 from Highwood Junction to the Kananaskis Lakes turnoff. As the area is an important corridor for wildlife, this road is barricaded each year from December 1 to June 15.

The trips east and north of the highway are generally shorter and benefit the most from snow-clearing Chinooks winds. Those west of the highway all lie on the Continental Divide. As such, their approaches are some of the longest in the book and they are the first to hold snow. Biking old logging roads helps to shorten the lengthy amount of time required for many of these mountains, especially on return. These mountains also are a magnet for clouds and the formation of clouds. You may find yourself in white-out like conditions on Mount Armstrong, while those on Mount Head at the same time enjoy clear, blue skies.

From the summit of Mount Loomis, looking south to the southern outlier of Loomis and Mount Bishop to the left.

Holy Cross Mountain 2,685 m

Difficulty Easy via east face, moderate via northeast ridge
Round-trip time 7–11 hours
Elevation gain 1,225 m
Maps 82 J/7 Mount Head, Gem Trek Highwood & Cataract Creek

Depending on the level of scrambling you desire, Holy Cross offers a couple of routes to its summit, from steep hiking to moderate scrambling. With the right snow conditions, the east face grants a superb glissade down. Otherwise, expect the usual fare of Rockies rubble and scree. Try from June on.

Park on the side of the road by Gunnery Creek. When heading west, this is approximately 1 km past the Sentinel Recreation turnoff. Find the trail on the right side of the creek and off you go (heading north), for several kilometres. Soon, the trail begins to drop. Follow it for several minutes and then leave the trail, heading northwest and aiming for a grassy hill. From the hill, both ascent routes are visible. The northeast route offers better and more interesting scrambling and is recommended for ascent. The east face can then be used for descent.

To tackle the northeast route, drop down to the creek from the hill, cross the water, and then head up the other side through light forest. Once above the tree line, a rock band is visible that can be circumvented by trending to

The ascent routes from the hill. NE northeast ridge. S summit. D east face and descent route.

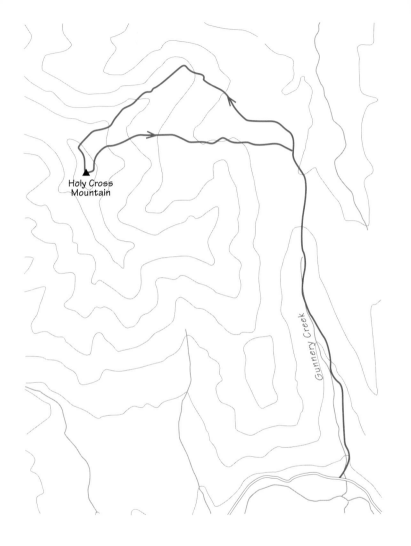

Holy Cross
Mountain

Gunnery Creek

the right. This will put you at the lower end of the northeast ridge. Follow the ridge, enjoying various degrees of scrambling to the summit ridge. Steeper rock bands can be circumvented on the left side.

Once on the summit ridge, turn left and follow the sometimes narrow and mildly exposed ridge to the summit. If a strong west wind is blowing, this traverse may be "exciting." The summit panorama features a comprehensive view of the Continental Divide peaks of the southern Kananaskis area, from Mount Odlum all the way down to Pierce and beyond. Mount Head (another worthwhile scramble) sits to the northwest and is connected to Holy Cross by a narrow ridge.

Return the same way or descend the much easier east face. If snow conditions are good, and you are skilled at glissading and self-arrest, a great deal of elevation can be lost in minutes. At the bottom, follow the drainage, looking for the hill you started from. Lower down, stay on the right side of the valley to avoid unnecessary elevation loss and regain, and make your way back to the hill and then back down to Gunnery Trail.

Mount Head 2,782 m

Difficulty Moderate with one difficult step via east ridge; moderate
    via southeast slopes
Round-trip time 9–12 hours
Elevation gain 1,500 m
Maps 82 J/7 Mount Head, Gem Trek Highwood & Cataract Creek

Mount Head is one of the higher peaks of the Highwood Range and is a fine objective (the highest at GR571013 is unnamed, although it is sometimes referred to as Highwood Peak). The east ridge of Mount Head provides splendid scenery and its front-range location makes early- and late-season ascents possible. Try from June on.

Park at Sentinel lot on Highway 546. Hike a couple of hundred metres back up the road, heading east. Cross to the north side and find the Grass Pass trailhead. A 3.2-km hike takes you to the pass, at which point you'll start to lose elevation as you keep heading north on the wide trail. An occasional glance to the left should give you a decent view of the route you will be taking.

After several kilometers, the trail suddenly drops sharply down to the left, and you arrive at a meadow. Two routes exist from this point.

Route 1–Difficult East Ridge: Head northwest across the meadow and find the creek that originates from the valley, south of the mountain. Cross the creek

The ascent route from the trail. C crux. 1 first high point. 2 second high point. S summit. ED easy descent route.

and hike up easy slopes to the start of the treed ridge. Once on the ridge, turn left and head directly west. It undulates in a couple of places, but eventually you will arrive at a clearing with the ascent route visible straight ahead (see photo above).

Ascend treed slopes just left of centre to circumvent the first outcrop of vertical rock. Once around the band, it is best to veer right and ascend alongside it. At the top, head straight toward the cliff bands and then traverse left around the band to find an obvious weakness. Ascend the weakness to a small plateau. Now for the crux—finding a feasible way up the second rock band. From the plateau, hike up to the face of the rock band and traverse left below its vertical walls. If snow remains here, a slip might launch you over the cliffs below unless you can self-arrest immediately—in this case, crampons and an ice axe are mandatory. Another option is to turn around and look for another route. Turn a corner and the crux step should be right in front of you—a 5-m, near vertical step, with trees at the top (see photo on p. 121). Initially, the step may look easy; however, upon starting the ascent you may find it more challenging than it appears. There are few goods holds and more than likely, near the top, you will find yourself grabbing for tree branches and hoping they will hold your weight should you slip. Once you start up, it will be difficult to back down, so be sure of your decision to ascend this step. If you don't like the looks of this crux step, there are easier places to ascend the rock band. This will, however, require you to descend back through the weakness and then traverse

The crux step.

around the left side of the band to look for a viable route up. You may have to lose a fair amount of elevation before one becomes apparent.

After the crux, the remainder of the ascent is significantly easier and the scenery improves dramatically as you gain elevation. Though it is possible to avoid unnecessary elevation losses and gains by side-sloping the south side of the east ridge more or less directly to the summit, this route is tedious and means you will miss out on some of the more interesting scrambling and scenery that the mountain has to offer. I recommend you stay on the east ridge throughout and visit every high point along the way. The first significant high point is easily ascended and descended and doesn't require a great deal of extra time. The second will require you to head left and down to circumvent an airy drop-off on the north side of the ridge, but it is well worth a quick visit. After this second high point, regain the ridge and continue up toward the summit. At the top, enjoy the pleasant contrast of the shapely peaks to the north, south, and west, with the foothills and prairies to the east.

Route 2—Moderate Southeast Slopes: At the meadow, head northwest and find the creek that originates from the valley south of the mountain. Follow the creek on its left side for approximately 2 km. Once past the first major drainage, turn right and ascend steep, treed slopes in a northwest direction. Once above the tree line, the route becomes clear. The summit is way over to the left and can be reached more or less in a direct line by side-sloping the south face. That said, it is preferable (and certainly more interesting) to gain the east ridge and follow it to the summit—see the route described after the crux above.

Several return routes exist. You could return via the east ridge. You must be confident that you can downclimb the crux (or rappel, if you have the necessary equipment). Don't try this descent route if you didn't come up this way. You could also return via the southeast slopes (the moderate route in reverse to avoid the crux). Descend the east ridge until is it feasible to turn right, then head in a southeast direction to the tree line. You'll want to stay to well right of the major drainage on your left. The route is fairly tedious due to the rubble. At tree line, continue down to the valley, where you will turn left and hike down the valley to rejoin the creek.

A third return option is to descend via southwest slopes and Stony Creek. This route offers a quick way off the mountain, though bushwhacking alongside Stony Creek can be tedious and very time consuming. From the summit, start down the obvious gully on the southwest side of the mountain. As you lose elevation, trend right over several ribs to find the gully that leads straight down to the valley bottom. Other gullies lead to drop-offs, so finding the correct gully is imperative. Once in the valley, there is only one way to go— down and due south. Follow Stony Creek out to the highway, turn left, and walk back to your car, about 4 km away.

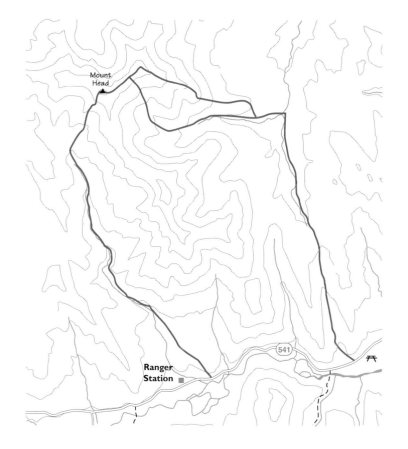

Mount Head

541

Ranger Station

"Lineham Creek Peaks" 2,716 m to 2,775 m

Difficulty Moderate via northwest ridge to GR618951, mild exposure; difficult to GR628936, with considerable exposure—a climber's scramble
Round-trip time 5–7 for GR618951; add 2 hours for GR628936
Elevation gain 1,150 m to GR618951; add 200 m for GR628936
Maps 82 J/7 Mount Head, Gem Trek Highwood & Cataract Creek

Though the Highwood Range is home to more than 25 distinct peaks, only five of them have been named. This trip allows you to visit 1–4 of those without a name. The first three are relatively straightforward, however, the fourth involves difficult scrambling with plenty of significant exposure and should only be attempted by experienced scramblers. Inaccessible from December 1 to mid-June. Try from mid-June on.

Park at Lineham Creek Parking lot, 12.1 km north of the Highway 40/940 junction. The Lineham Creek Trail starts at the back of the parking lot. Hike the trail as it goes up, down, and then eventually crosses the creek twice. Use rocks or logs to ford the creeks. About 100 m after the second crossing, the trail

The ascent route seen from the trail. S summit of GR618951. LS lower summit at GR616953. ED easy descent route.

splits. Both end up in the same place, but the left is more defined. This trail leaves the creek and then curves back toward it in short order. If you find yourself moving farther away from the creek and up, you might be headed up Lineham Ridge—back up and find the correct trail, which parallels the creek.

Hike the trail for several more kilometres. Right before the third and final creek crossing of the day, the objective comes into view—the right and slightly higher of two peaks to the northwest (see photo on p. 124). Cross the creek and continue on the trail as it ascends onto a bench and then along the bench's right side. When the terrain opens up a little and it becomes obvious to do so, trend right to gain the lower slopes of the objective. The left peak is also feasible, but is closer to steep hiking than scrambling. Once on the correct slope, ascend it all the way to the top, staying on the ridge throughout. Higher up the scrambling begins. For the best scrambling, choose enjoyable slabs instead of tedious scree. The terrain does get steeper toward the top and may be considered mildly exposed by some hikers.

The summit grants a comprehensive view of the Continental Divide peaks of southern Kananaskis. Mount McPhail is the noticeable triangular-shaped peak and one of seven mountains in the Rockies loosely classified as a "Pyramid." The 11,000er Mount Harrison will be visible behind Mount Muir on a clear day. Abruzzi and Joffre dominate farther north and even distant King George can be picked out.

Of more immediate concern, however, are the ridges that extend from the summit in either direction. If satiated, **return** the same way, though the northwest extension offers an easier descent. The northwest extension to GR616953 is a simple ridgewalk with a narrow, exposed section right before the summit. The rock is loose here, so check all hand- and footholds carefully. From the summit, follow the easier ridge (paralleling the one you ascended to GR618951) to the valley below, where it eventually intersects the trail.

A more extensive and considerably more challenging option goes all the way to GR628936, and offers a chance to nab GR623946 on the way. GR628936 is the second highest point of the southern section of the Highwood Range, surpassed in height only by Mount Head. This route is only for experienced scramblers who are comfortable with long sections of exposed scrambling on less-than-solid rock. Make sure the tread on your boots (or approach shoes) is in good condition—you'll need it!

Continue south over to GR623946 without difficulty. As always, stay on the ridge as much as possible. From this summit, lose a fair amount of elevation to a low point between GR623946 and your objective. The ridge starts to narrow even more and then drops down again. Before this drop, it is better to back up a little and descend in order to circumvent this entire section (see photo on p. 126). Traverse easier terrain until a clear route back to the ridge

Ascent route to GR628936. C crux.

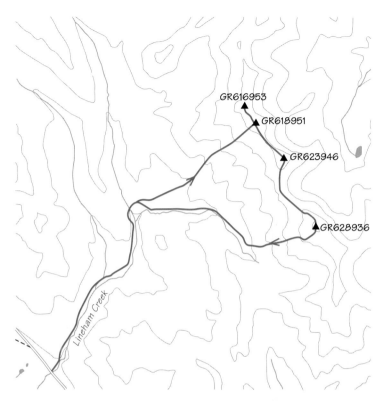

becomes visible, just before a major slab on the west face. Do not regain the ridge too early as this detour will take you around the steepest section of the ridge. Once back on the ridge, follow it to the summit. This section is longer than you may think, very exposed, and the rock is not always solid—go slowly and carefully, as any slip would be fatal.

At the summit, newly named Patterson's Peak lies to the east, while Mount Head sits farther south along the ridge. Assuming you have no desire to downclimb the ridge you just came up, descend the west ridge directly from the summit until you arrive at a dirt/scree slope on the right side of the ridge (dark dirt, not the light brown scree slope). Descend this easy but tedious slope all the way down to the valley. Keep going down and to the right toward the creek. Follow the creek out to where it joins up with the trail. Head home.

Lineham Ridge 2,698 m and
GR593982–East Peak 2,807 m

Difficulty Moderate via northwest ridge; some exposure
Round-trip time 4.5–6 for Lineham; 6–8 for GR593982
Elevation gain 950 m to Lineham; add 280 m for GR593982
Maps 82 J/7 Mount Head, 82 J/10 Mount Rae, Gem Trek Highwood
& Cataract Creek

The summit of Lineham Ridge can be easily reached via a good hiking trail along its southeast ridge. The northwest ridge of the mountain, however, provides interesting scrambling on good rock. As well, a higher summit to the east can be added on to the day, with an easy descent route that takes you alongside all four of the popular and scenic Picklejar Lakes. A good candidate for the use of approach shoes —on ascent anyway! Inaccessible from December 1 to June 15. Try mid-June on.

The ascent route. S summit of Lineham Ridge.

Park at Lantern Creek parking lot, 17.4 km north of the Highway 40/940 junction. Hike north on the road for 50 or so metres and find the Picklejar Lakes Trail on the east side. Hike the trail for 4 km (about 50–60 minutes at a fast pace). Lineham Ridge appears in front of you and the route ascends the left skyline. As soon as the first Picklejar Lake becomes visible, leave the trail, to your right, and easily gain the ridge.

From here to the summit, for the best scrambling experience, you'll want to stay on the ridge throughout, even when it becomes steeper and appears to end in drop-offs. All are easily downclimbed or simply don't exist. Lower down, it is possible to circumvent steeper sections on either side of the ridge,

Typical terrain on the ridge.

but eventually that option disappears so you might as well get used to the terrain. The rock is surprisingly solid and easy to grip in most sections. Approach shoes lend themselves very well to the terrain, however, boots with a good tread are fine also.

The ridge is deceivingly long and a cairn placed at a false summit might be somewhat of an annoyance. Continue past this cairn and make your way to the obvious high point. If you've had enough, enjoy the panorama and **return** the same way, or for an easier descent, head south to the next (and much lower) high point (one exposed section). A trail then heads down, in a north-west direction, eventually joining up with the Picklejar Lakes Trail.

The extension to a higher summit at GR593982 to the east is worthwhile for several reasons. It affords one the added view of the Dogtooth Mountains to the east. It allows for an easier descent route and a chance to visit the scenic Picklejar Lakes. It's higher!

The actual scrambling falls short of that which you've just come up and mostly amounts to a rubble ascent. Head east, losing 80 m of elevation to a grassy col and start up the other side. Again, stay close to the edge to get the best experience. Like Lineham, there are a few false summits. The high point has a cairn and the best view. The alternate descent is far from aesthetic, but

The route to GR593982 and alternate descent route. S summit.

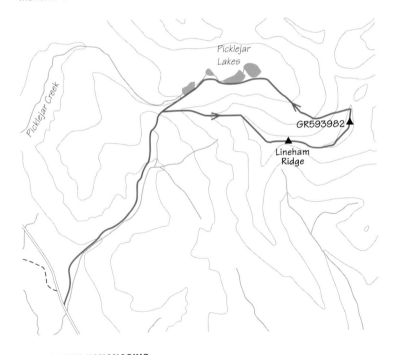

is it shorter, easier, and more scenic. Continue along the ridge for a short distance, looking for an obvious ramp to the left. Here the scree is a light shade of brown. Unfortunately, this slope is all rubble and offers little in terms of good scree surfing. If you're wearing approach shoes, you'll be hating life for the next 45 minutes. At the bottom, work your way over to the banks of the south side of the fourth Picklejar Lake and find the trail that takes you effortlessly past all of the lakes and back to the parking lot.

Gibraltar Mountain 2,665 m

Difficulty Moderate via Mist Ridge and west slopes
Round-trip time 12–15 hours
Elevation gain 1,700–2,000 m (depending on return route)
Maps 82 J/10 Mount Rae, Gem Trek Highwood & Cataract Creek

A long but enjoyable scramble in beautiful surroundings. Be prepared for approximately 2 full kilometers of elevation gain, by the time you have negotiated the ups and downs of Mist Ridge. Inaccessible from December 1 to June 15. Try between June 15 and November 30 in dry years.

Start from Mist Creek parking lot on the west side of Highway 40. Find the trail at the north end of the parking lot and follow it across Highway 40, continuing on the trail on the other side. After 50 m, take a right, then a left and hike the wide trail for 2 km. At the Mist Creek intersection, take the right-

Mist Ridge and Gibraltar Mountain, seen from the south summit of Mist Ridge. MS summit of Mist Ridge. S summit of Gibraltar.

hand trail, which eventually leads to the south summit of Mist Ridge. Follow the undulating ridge to the north summit, taking in beautiful views of Mist Mountain and Storm Mountain to west, and your destination ahead and to the right.

From the north summit, descend east-facing slopes to the Mist Ridge/ Gibraltar Mountain col and start up the other side. Travel a little to the left as you ascend in order to gain the ridge as soon as possible. Once on the ridge, stay there and traverse enjoyable terrain toward the summit, which is incorrectly identified on some maps. The tilted orientation of the rock leads to a few drop-offs, which may or may not be downclimbable, depending on any snow or ice remaining on the rock. If not downclimbable, lose elevation to the right and traverse around these obstacles. One obstacle may require a fair loss of elevation to circumvent.

From the true summit, it looks awfully tempting to continue east, down the ridge to the lower summit. The northeast face of this summit boasts a remarkable, 800-m vertical climb, completed in eight grueling days by Bill Davidson and Jim White in 1971. In the equally remarkable event that you have both the time and energy to complete the descent, head down the ridge, traversing right when needed. Just remember, once you get there, it's a long, long way back to your car and the return trip will involve several significant elevation gains. **Return** the same way.

Kevin Barton enjoys typical scrambling on the ridge.

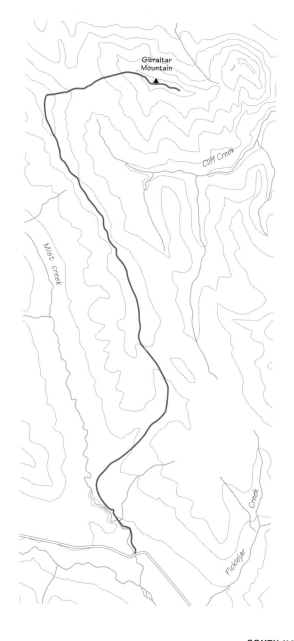

Gibraltar
Mountain

Cliff Creek

Mist creek

Picklejar Creek

Picklejar

Mount Odlum 2,716 m

Difficulty Moderate via north ridge
Round-trip time 6–8 hours
Elevation gain 840 m
Maps 82 J/10 Mount Rae , 82 J/7 Mount Head, Gem Trek Highwood
& Cataract Creek

Mount Odlum will not be winning the "Scramble of the Year" award, but it is rel-atively short when compared to its neighbours to the south and grants a good view of the valley to the west and the Italian Group. The route described below is best if you intend to summit Odlum only. If Loomis is also in your plans, use the Loomis/Odlum description (Route 2). Inaccessible from December 1 to June 15. Try from late July on.

Park on the south side of Highway 40, just after a rail-guard, 29.5 km south of the Kananaskis Lakes Trail turnoff or 12.3 km south of the Highwood Pass sign. Odlum is visible to the southwest, between two treed ridges. The object is to ascend the valley between these ridges to the northeast side of Odlum. From the road, descend to Storm Creek and cross (ford) it. The crux of the trip

The ascent from the meadows northeast of the summit. R the scree ramp.

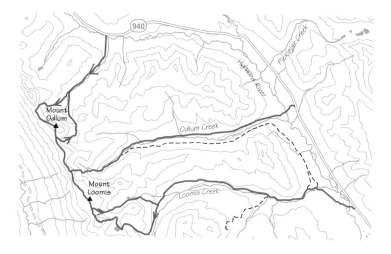

follows—finding the trail. As long as you are heading in a southwest direction, you'll run into the trail or an abundance of flagging sooner or later—follow either. They both eventually lead to the unmaintained but distinct trail. Follow this trail for several kilometres and cross a small stream. Stay right after the stream and follow another trail to more open meadows. The trail disappears in the long grass here. Wade through the grass to another meadow, where the entire ascent route should be visible.

The key to gaining the col northwest of Odlum is an obvious rubble ramp far to the right. It may look steep from the meadow, and, in fact, it is in places, but still requires only easy to moderate scrambling to ascend. Work your way over to the ramp and start up. Getting up the ramp is very tedious. Sticking to the right sides allows you to use the rock walls to help, but it is still a grunt. A snow patch just before the col may persist well into July. Move onto the rock on the right if this is the case or step-kick up the snow if you have an ice axe.

From the col head southeast and follow the ridge to the summit of Odlum. There are a couple of mildly exposed moves right near the beginning, but it's mostly easy ridgewalking after that. Be careful when walking on the west side of the ridge—you'll be in BC and may be subject to their Provincial Sales Tax (PST). Hop over to the east side of the ridge (back into Alberta) if anyone tries to sell you something! Just before the summit the terrain gets steeper. Either scramble straight up the ridge or avoid the steep part by going around it on the right side.

If you've completed other scrambles of the southern section of the Elk Range, the summit view might be a little repetitive, but is satisfying nonetheless. Rather than retracing your steps, a much easier **return** route exists on the southeast side of the peak in the form of rubble slopes. Head down the south ridge for a few minutes until the slope becomes clear. Follow it down to the valley, trending left to find a trail, heading northeast, at the bottom. You now have to swing around the east side of the mountain to get back into the correct valley. Be careful that you don't descend into the valley directly east of Odlum—it will take you back to the road, but more than 8 km away from your vehicle. Once in the correct valley, return the way you came.

Mount Loomis 2,822 m

Difficulty Moderate from the north; difficult from the south
Round-trip time 9–12 hours, depending on route; add 5 hours if also
  ascending Odlum
Elevation gain 1,200–1,400 m
Maps 82 J/7 Mount Head, Gem Trek Highwood & Cataract Creek

There are at least three feasible routes to this summit. The most challenging and interesting of the three (Route 1) goes first to Loomis Lake and then to the southern outlier of Loomis, before reaching the true summit. Route 2 is best if you also plan to summit Mount Odlum on the same trip and gives you the choice of both or either one of the two summits. See Mount Odlum for the third route. Expect at least a 14-hour day to do both mountains. Inaccessible from December 1 to June 15. Try from July on.

Route 1—Difficult via Loomis Creek Trail: This is a climber's scramble; a bike approach is recommended. Park on the east side of Highway 40, 1.2 km north of the Lineham Creek parking lot. Cross the road, hop the guardrail, and descend grassy slopes to a wide trail heading north, arriving at the Highwood River within a few minutes. Hip-waders are highly recommended, not only for the ford of the Highwood, but also for the numerous creek crossings after. Ford the river and find the wide Loomis Creek Trail on the other side. Bike (or hike) the trail for approximately 1 km, at which point it crosses Loomis Creek. Cross the creek and take the trail on the left, as it heads uphill. Follow the trail for another 6.2 km, leaving your bike at the end of an open meadow. Allow 1.5–2 hours from the car to the meadow by bike. The trail starts to degrade here and is often wet and muddy. Eventually it runs right into Loomis Creek and then ascends alongside it. Follow it into more open terrain (popular camping site) and trend left either following the trail as it weaves its way uphill, or head more directly west to the lake.

You'll certainly want to take a break at beautiful Loomis Lake to enjoy the

Difficult route. The southern outlier of Loomis from Loomis Lake. Ascent route is approximate.

wonderful surroundings. Take special note of the prominent outlier northwest of the lake—that's where you'll be going. The route basically ascends steep rubble slopes above the lake toward several rows of striking pinnacles and rock formations. Though it is not necessary to ascend all the way to the ridge, this route does give you the best scenery, an option to bail out on the difficult route by taking the easy one on the other side of the outlier, and maximizes your route options up the southeast face of the outlier.

Depending on where you top out on the ridge, you will have to hike a few metres or a few hundred metres up the ridge before you arrive at a steep rock band that is not within the realm of scrambling. Lose elevation on the left to circumvent this band and then gain it back while traversing up and across. This is the pattern you will be following to reach the 2,743-m summit of the outlier. A detailed description here would be too complicated. Route-find your way up and across the face, looking for the path of least resistance—even the easiest route will require some intense and exposed scrambling. Again, this is a route for experienced scramblers/climbers, with good route-finding abilities. If you are not confident about ascending steep, loose, exposed terrain, with the occasional lower-fifth-class move (and downclimbing that same terrain), this is not a good route choice for you.

At the summit of the outlier, the route to Loomis is clear. Descend one of a few gullies to the northwest for about 50 m and then traverse back east to the ridge. Descending the ridge is easy, though you wouldn't want to slip to the right! From the low col, a 250-vertical m and 25-minute slog takes you easily to the summit. Hug the ridge for the best scenery. Just above the col, take note of the cairn that marks the optional and easy descent route.

If you didn't bike Loomis Creek Trail, there is the option to continue north to a couple of outliers between Loomis and Odlum and then on to the summit of the latter. This makes for a very long day and will leave you a great distance from your car (see optional route descriptions for Loomis and Odlum to investigate routes for return). Most will **return** via Little Loomis Lake. Descend the way you came, almost to the col, and then work your way down onto steep scree slopes east of the col. Unfortunately, the terrain here is hard and not good for scree surfing, but it leads easily to the valley below and Little Loomis Lake. Find a trail on the right (south) side of the lake and follow it down to where it intersects with Loomis Creek Trail. If you lose the trail, just go southeast and down, through the bush. Eventually you'll run into Loomis Creek Trail. Turn left onto it and go home.

Route 2—Moderate via Odlum Creek Trail: Park at Lantern Creek parking lot, 17.4 km north of the Highway 40/940 junction. Hike a few hundred metres north up the highway, looking for a large boulder that marks the start of the Odlum Creek Trail. Follow the trail as it drops down to the Highwood River. Carefully cross the river (runners or hip-waders) and find the cutline (trail) on the other side. The cutline parallels Odlum Creek for the next 7.5 km (go straight at all intersections), eventually leading to Odlum Pond. Mount Loomis towers above you, while the summit of Odlum is, for now, blocked by its slightly lower southern outlier.

From Odlum Pond, the objective is to gain the outlier immediately north of Loomis (GR468932). Circle around the south side of the pond and cross the creek, aiming for the right side of the watercourse—the least steep route. Above the waterfalls, cross the creek again and continue up toward the col between Loomis and GR468932. Pass under the steep walls of GR468932, looking right to ascend the first gully, a route that leads to the east ridge. Scramble up the ridge to the first of four possible summits you may achieve in the day.

After enjoying views of Sir Douglas and Joffre to the northwest and Mount Abruzzi due west, turn south and follow the easy to moderate ridge to the summit of Loomis. If Loomis is your only goal, **return** the same way. If you miraculously have the energy to also bag Odlum, return to the col and continue north along the ridge, first to the southern outlier of Odlum and then to

Moderate route. The route to GR468932, from Odlum Pond. O Odlum Pond. GR GR468932.

Odlum itself. Use the easier descent route outlined in the Mount Odlum description or **return** the same way. The former means avoiding additional elevation gains, but this descent may be trickier since you didn't come up this way, and it will also leave you about 8 km from your car once you reach the highway.

Mount Bishop 2,850 m

Difficulty Moderate via southeast slopes
Round-trip time 7–10 hours
Elevation gain 1,200 m
Maps 82 J/7 Mount Head, Gem Trek Highwood & Cataract Creek

Bishop is a little closer to the road than it's neighbours to the north and south (Loomis and McPhail respectively) but still requires a lengthy approach. Old logging roads and good trails make the approach an easy one, and if you are unable to summit Mount Bishop, Bishop's Ridge makes for a fine alternative trip. Inaccessible from December 1 to June 15. Try from July on.

Park on the east side of Highway 40, 1.2 km north of the Lineham Creek parking lot. Cross the road, hop the guardrail, and descend grassy slopes to a wide trail heading north, arriving at the Highwood River within a few minutes. Hipwaders are highly recommended, not only for the ford of the Highwood, but also for the numerous creek crossings after. Ford the river and find the wide Loomis Creek Trail on the other side. Bike or hike the trail for approximately 1 km, at which point it crosses Loomis Creek. Cross the creek and take the trail on the left as it heads uphill. Four more crossings of Loomis Creek follow.

The southeast slopes and ascent route of Bishop from Loomis Creek Trail.

The key rock band to look for. R rock band.

About 100 m after the fifth river crossing (fourth of Loomis Creek in total) the grassy and unsigned Bishop Creek Trail veers off to the left. Leave your bike here and start along Bishop Creek Trail, which crosses Loomis Creek yet again almost immediately (the last crossing of the day).

Follow the trail as it slowly gains elevation above Bishop Creek. Soon the view begins to open up, with Bishop Ridge in front and Mount Bishop to its left. Stay on the trail as the trail traverses the south slopes of Bishop Ridge. Before you know it, the daunting east face of Mount Bishop is right in front of you. Now you must swing left (south), over to the southeast side of the mountain. Lose a little elevation and then trudge up scree slopes to the shoulder. Now looking at the southeast face of the mountain. It may appear that you can go straight up the ridge. Beware: much of the terrain on this slope is much steeper than it looks from afar. As well, the rock is loose and down-sloping and therefore an easier route farther south and then west along the face is recommended.

Traverse scree slopes to the left around the south side of the mountain, looking up to your right for a distinctive band of rock that is the key to the ascent (see photo above). After several hundred metres of traversing, head up to the left side of the rock band and an obvious weakness. Scramble easily up the weakness, arriving at a steeper band that doesn't look too bad but is more challenging than you might think. Descend left alongside the band to find a more feasible route up.

Once above this band, the terrain and route-finding become a little easier.

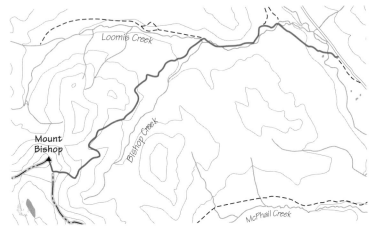

Ascend the face, trending right as you go, always looking for the path of least resistance (moderate scrambling at most). If the rock is dry, more challenging routes with steep hands-on scrambling are certainly feasible. Arrive at the ridge and plod to the summit, a short distance away.

The view is splendid, even if you have completed nearby ascents of McPhail or Loomis, which lie respectively to the south and north. **Return** the same way. If by any chance you have 400 vertical m of elevation left in you, head up scenic Bishop Ridge, directly east of Mount Bishop on the way back. The ridge is home to some wonderful rock scenery and is a terrific viewpoint in itself.

Mount McPhail 2,865 m

Difficulty Easy via southeast ridge; moderate via south slopes
Round-trip time 8–11 hours, with a bike approach; add 4 hours if also ascending Mount Muir
Elevation gain 1,290 m
Maps 82 J/7 Mount Head, Gem Trek Highwood & Cataract Creek

Don't let a long bike approach deter you from attempting this beautiful mountain in wonderful surroundings. Success may depend upon the condition of the lengthy McPhail Creek trail and the water level of the Highwood River, so don't try it too early. Inaccessible from December 1 to June 15. Try from July on.

Mount McPhail and the long route via McPhail Creek.

Park at the Cat Creek parking lot, 5.6 km north of the Highway 40/940 junction. Start from the northwest end of the parking lot, following a wide trail that parallels the Highwood River. Cross the Highwood River at about the 2.3-km mark (hip-waders are a luxury here, but runners will do) and continue on. Stay on the trail throughout, or take the regular shortcuts to the left on more narrow trails to avoid excess elevation gains and losses. Hopefully the trail will be dry and relatively easy to negotiate. If wet and muddy, the 10-km ride might well be the crux of the trip. After heading more or less in a northwest direction, the trail eventually turns west, heading toward Mount McPhail. Don't change your footwear yet, as several streams interrupt the trail.

Eventually you will arrive at the headwall, with Mount McPhail to the right and Mount Muir to the left. Ditch your bike and start ascending the headwall to the right of the waterfall. If you have lost the trail, don't despair—you'll run into it as long as you are going up. At the top of the headwall is a shallow tarn, backdropped beautifully by Mount McPhail. If doing an overnighter, this area would provide a great bivy site. The route up McPhail starts to be become obvious at this point—more so as you head farther west on the trail.

The fastest way up ascends scree slopes on the east side of the south face. Staying near the edge provides great views to the east. If you are looking for a

Approaching the headwall. H headwall. S summit.

The south and southeast slopes. S scramble route. SE easier southeast route.

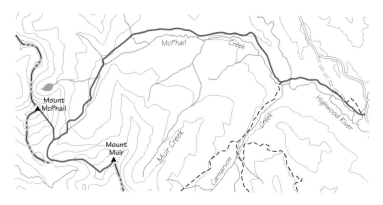

more challenging route with hands-on scrambling, keep heading west and ascend the centre gully of the south face up numerous rock bands. If you arrive at a section that is too difficult, traverse right (east) toward easier terrain. The summit is at the top of the gully.

Hopefully, you'll be blessed with clear skies to enjoy a magnificent summit panorama: Bishop and Loomis to the north; the Highwood Range to the east; 11,000ers Joffre, King George, and Harrison; and a beautiful sea of more Continental Divide Peaks to the south. The entire route up Mount Muir is also plainly visible. The east side of the south face provides the fastest descent route and if the snow conditions are good (assuming there is any snow) a long and exhilarating glissade may be possible. **Return** the same way.

Mount Muir 2,743 m

Difficulty Easy via west slopes
Round-trip time 8–11 hours, with a bike approach; add 4 hours if also ascending Mount McPhail
Elevation gain 1,170 m
Maps 82 J/7 Mount Head, Gem Trek Highwood & Cataract Creek

Given the long approach, it is best to try and summit both Mounts McPhail and Muir in a single trip. This does make for a very long and physically strenuous day and success may depend upon the negotiability of the McPhail Creek Trail. Leave early. Inaccessible from December 1 to June 15. Try from July on.

Park at the Cat Creek parking lot and follow the approach directions for Mount McPhail. At the tarn above the headwall, continue on the trail, heading southwest to the high point at Weary Creek Gap. Turn 90 degrees to the

The west ridge ascent route of Muir, as seen from the lower slopes of McPhail. S summit.

left and head up the wide and easy west ridge. The route curves a little to the south as you reach the false summit and then heads northeast to the true summit. **Return** the same way.

Mount Strachan 2,682 m

Difficulty Easy via south ridge
Round-trip time 8–11 hours (with a bike approach)
Elevation gain 1,120 m
Maps 82 J/7 Mount Head, Gem Trek Highwood & Cataract Creek

Even if you come up short of Mount Strachan's summit, this trip takes you, in exciting fashion, to the gorgeous blue waters of Carnarvon Lake. Consider the summit icing on the cake. Strachan is a little lower than its neighbours, but it still sports a terrific view. Again, the ascent involves a lengthy bike approach. Inaccessible from December 1 to June 15. Try from July on.

Park at the Cat Creek parking lot, 5.6 km north of the Highway 40/940 junction. Starting from the northwest end of the parking lot, bike or hike the wide

Approaching the headwall.

trail that parallels the Highwood River. Cross the Highwood River at about the 2.3-km mark (hip-waders keep you dry here, but runners will do) and continue on. Several hundred metres after crossing the river, take the left branch where the trail forks (the unmarked Carnarvon Lake Trail). It goes down a hill, crosses a stream, and then continues on a little to the right. This trail is popular with those on horseback—remember to get off your bike to pass or let pass when you run into these magnificent animals and their riders.

The trail forks again 2.9 km later. Take the right fork (marked with a cairn) and continue in a southwest direction for 4.5 km to the headwall. For cyclists, this part of the trail starts off okay, but several kilometres from the headwall it becomes steep and rocky. When this happens, it is best to ditch your bike and continue on foot.

Around the lake and up the southwest ridge.

At the headwall, enjoy the beautiful upper waterfall cascading down and then ascend the headwall using the chains on the right side of the fall. Continue easily to reach stunning Carnarvon Lake in minutes. Strachan is to your right and the ascent route goes up the left skyline starting at the west end of the lake. Walk around the lake on the right side and gain the ridge above the west end of the lake (see photo above). From here, turn right and embark on an easy scree slog to the summit (hiking poles are useful here). Any route will do, but staying right will at least keep the lake within your field of vision for the longest amount of time. Also, the east face does have a few interesting pinnacles to admire. Near the top, the ridge turns to the west and the summit is reached shortly after.

The southwest ridge route.

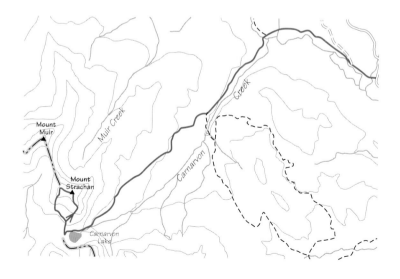

On a clear day, the view boasts a couple 11,000ers (Harrison and the southeast side of Joffre), Mount Abruzzi to the west, and an unrestricted view of the entire Highwood Range. Mount MacLaren lies to the south, while Muir and McPhail are immediately north. A quick stroll to the north summit of Strachan gives an even better view of Muir.

While it is tempting to continue north to Mount Muir, this requires a steep descent to the col on dangerously loose rubble and also involves a very steep downclimb with few good holds. This route is not recommended. Another option is to descend almost all the way back to Carnarvon Lake, turn north to gain the southwest ridge of Muir, and continue to the summit. This route is not difficult, however, it is lengthy and tedious and again is not recommended. The summit of Muir is best reached via the McPhail Creek approach. **Return** the same way, or head down rubble slopes toward the valley to the southwest pretty much at any place from the summit ridge. There are a few large towers of rock that are worth checking out on the southwest side of the mountain.

Mount Armstrong 2,804 m

Difficulty Moderate via south and southwest ridge; some exposure
Round-trip time 10–14 hours
Elevation gain 1,200 m
Maps 82 J/7 Mount Head, Gem Trek Highwood & Cataract Creek

Mount Armstrong is a long distance from the road, however, an old logging road that parallels Baril Creek makes relatively short work of the approach, especially if you are riding a bike. The environs of the Fording Pass area are superb and the summit view is stunning. For a two-peak day, nearby Mount Bolton is an easy ascent. Try from mid-June on.

From Longview, drive west on Highway 541 and turn left onto the 940 at Highwood Junction. Drive for 3.3 km and park on the right side of the road in a small clearing. Follow a trail on the right (north) side of the clearing, that leads to the Baril Creek Trail within a few minutes. Hike or bike (preferable) the trail for 6.9 km until you arrive at the first of several creek crossings, marked by an "ICY TRAIL AHEAD" sign. Cross Baril Creek on two logs to your left. When you reach the second "ICY TRAIL AHEAD" sign, take a trail that heads off to the right. This route bypasses a couple of the subsequent creek crossings. The trail eventually descends to an open area. Continue west until you run into the creek again. If you are riding a bike, this is a good place to ditch it and continue on foot (GR616784). Cross the creek and continue on

The route up the westerly south ridge of Armstrong. S summit.

for approximately 500 m, then cross the creek for a third time. Look for a sign on the right side of the trail that reads "GDT north" at GR612778. Take this trail and follow it up and west. It eventually joins up with a wider trail that takes you up to the beautiful and open terrain south of Armstrong. To the south lies Baril Peak, Mount Cornwell, and several outliers of those peaks. Mount Bolton is due west. U-shaped Mount Armstrong has two south ridges and you will be ascending the more westerly one.

Continue west until the westerly south ridge becomes visible to the northwest (see photo above). The trail continues to a col between Bolton and the southwest ridge of Armstrong, but it is quicker to leave it here and ascend a ridge on the right directly to the south ridge. On the way, you will be required to lose a little elevation and cross a small creek. Gain Armstrong's south ridge at about GR587782 and follow it north to a great viewpoint southwest of the true summit. This slope is foreshortened and may take longer than you think. It will, however, also net you all but 100 m of the remaining elevation gain of the day.

Provided you are blessed with clear skies, the 1-km ridgewalk to the true summit is probably the best part of the trip. Follow the ridge throughout, carefully downclimbing several steps along the way. The ridge is narrow and exposed for a few short sections. After taking in the superb summit panorama, **return** the same way. Tagging Mount Bolton to the southwest is an easy affair. Add approximately 500 m of elevation gain and about 2.5–3.5 hours to your day. Bolton also makes a good alternate ascent if you're not up for Armstrong. Descend to the Bolton/Armstrong col and then head up the easy northeast slopes to a fine viewpoint. **Return** the same way.

The northern section of Kananaskis extends as far north as the Canmore area. Many of the peaks in this section are much closer to the road (primarily Highways 1, 40, 742, and the Powderface Trail) and are therefore shorter and do not require the lengthy approaches of their southern counterparts. As well, these peaks are the most likely to be snow-free early in the season and benefit from Chinook conditions.

Again, the northern section of Kananaskis Country is thoroughly documented and described in Gillean Daffern's, *Kananaskis Country Trail Guide, Volume 1.*

Geology

Not surprisingly, the geology of the north end of Kananaskis is very similar to that of South Kananaskis, described in the previous section. Though samples of good quality limestone may be more prevalent in the north end, the rock remains loose and largely unreliable. The west ridge of Mount Baldy's west peak is a notable exception, offering a difficult but very worthwhile scrambling experience on beautifully solid friction slabs. North Kananaskis is also home to one of the most striking and noticeable examples of rock folding in the Canadian Rockies. I imagine there are very few who have not looked with amazement at the obvious syncline (where the rock has been folded in a trough-like shape) on Mount Kidd's south face. This specific geological phenomena is readily viewed when driving north on Highway 40.

Access

From Calgary drive west on the Trans-Canada Highway. For access to peaks along the southern section of the Powderface Trail and the Elbow Valley (Bryant, Howard, Threepoint), turn south onto Highway 22 and follow it to the hamlet of Bragg Creek. Turn left at the four-way stop and then right onto Highway 66, when the 22 hits a T-intersection.

Tiara Peak is better accessed from the north section of the Powderface Trail. From the Trans-Canada take the Sibbald Flats turnoff onto Highway 68. Drive west and turn left onto the Powderface Trail.

Continuing along the Trans-Canada, the Highway 40 turnoff appears next and offers access to all the peaks along that road. Shortly after the Highway 40 turnoff, the Highway 1X turnoff provides access to the east peak of Wendell Mountain.

For the remainder of the peaks along the Smith-Dorrien Trail (Highway 742) access is via Canmore for peaks at the north end of the road, and via Highway 40 and the Kananaskis Lakes Trail turnoff for peaks at the south end.

Accommodation

The northern section of Kananaskis offers considerably more options for accommodation than South Kananaskis. Canmore is rife with motels, hotels, and lodges. Deeper into the mountains, the three lodges at Kananaskis Village appeal to those who may be looking for a more luxurious place to stay. Of course, as hearty scramblers, you and your party may be searching for the best campground in the best location. There are several right around Canmore, and the Mount Kidd RV Park, south on Highway 40, is very popular. Lakeshore campsites along the west side of Spray Lake take you away from the bustle of Canmore. Campgrounds at the Kananaskis Lakes lie in wonderful surroundings and seem more secluded, even though they are often relatively busy.

Elbow Valley

Tiara Peak	2,533 m	easy	page 157
Mount Bryant	2,629 m	easy/difficult	page 159
Mount Howard	2,777 m	easy	page 162
Threepoint Mountain	2,595 m	easy/moderate	page 165

These four peaks stand almost at the front of the front ranges and make great early- or late-season objectives. Three of them require a drive along the Powderface Trail. When dry, this gravel road is easily negotiated, however, it can be treacherous when icy. In those circumstances, a couple of steep hills might prove to be problematic and, as such, the road is best avoided. While the quickest driving route to Tiara Peak approaches from the north, Bryant, Howard, and Threepoint are all accessed from Bragg Creek and Highway 66. The access roads to all four peaks are closed from December 1 to May 15.

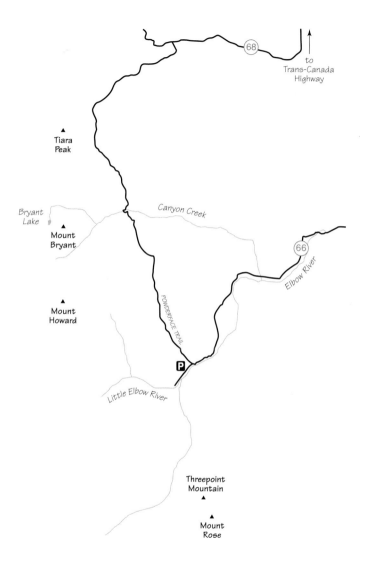

A snowy descent on Threepoint Mountain.

Tiara Peak 2,533 m

Difficulty Easy via north ridge and southwest slopes
Round-trip time 5–7 hours
Elevation gain 800 m
Maps 82 J/15 Bragg Creek, Gem Trek Canmore

Tiara Peak is the unofficial and descriptive name given to this peak that appropriately resembles a tiara when viewed from the north. There are plenty of routes to the summit ranging from easy scrambling to fourth-class climbing. The easiest route is described here. Can be easily combined with as ascent of Belmore Browne Peak. Inaccessible from December 1 to May 15. Try from mid-May on.

Drive to the Sibbald Flats turnoff and head south on Highway 68. At roughly the 23-km mark, turn left onto the Powderface Trail and follow it for 14.7 km before parking at the side of the road. Hike back along the road for about 100 m, looking for a trail on the west side. Follow the obvious trail along a cutline and past a large cut-block. Eventually the trail crosses a creek and then parallels the creek on the left side. Hike alongside the creek for about 10 minutes and then move into the middle and boulder hop your way up the creek until

The view from the Powderface Trail. BB Belmore Browne Peak. S summit of Tiara Peak. AD alternate descent.

it forks. Both forks will eventually take you to Tiara Peak, however, the right fork is best for ascent. The left fork is a good option for a quick and easy descent.

Follow the right-hand fork until above tree line and the scree slopes of Belmore Browne become visible. At this point, if Belmore Browne is your destination, keep following the creek and up scree slopes to the ridge. Turn right and head up to the summit of Belmore. To get directly to Tiara Peak, look to your left for steepish but easy slopes and head up to the ridge north of the peak. Ascend these slopes and turn left when you reach the ridge. A scenic ridgewalk follows, and soon you'll arrive at the crown of Tiara Peak—a steep and daunting-looking rock band.

Traverse along the base of the east (left) side of the summit block, around its south end, and then along the southwest side of the block. An easy route up soon reveals itself, though care should be exercised on the scree-on-slabs sections. Several cairns mark the route. **Return** the same way. Once back around the east side of the summit block, it is possible to descend east-facing slopes to a drainage below. Follow the drainage back to the original route.

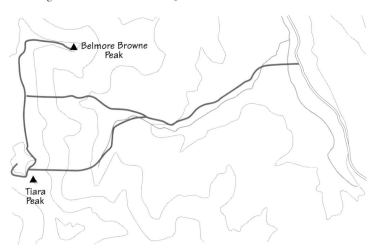

Mount Bryant 2,629 m

Difficulty Easy via northwest slopes; difficult traverse to lower east summit
Round-trip time 6.5–8 hours
Elevation gain 900 m
Maps 82 J/14 Spray Lakes Reservoir, 82 J/15 Bragg Creek, Gem Trek
    Canmore and Bragg Creek

The route for this mountain is the only one for which I recommend the easy route up and a more challenging route down. The day includes a visit to a beautiful tarn, a terrific summit view, a challenging traverse to the lower east summit, and a very entertaining alternate descent route. As such, it's strongly recommended you wait for a clear day to make the attempt. Inaccessible from December 1 to May 15. Try from June on. Summit at GR412407.

The east side of Mount Bryant as seen from Canyon Creek. E east summit. S true summit.

Drive west on Highway 66 and turn off (actually the road just goes straight) onto the Powderface Trail. Continue for 14.5 km and park in an open area where wide Canyon Creek meets the road (GR458419).

Hike along the wide, dried-up river bed for about 25 minutes. Bryant is in front of you to the right. Look for an obvious tributary coming in from the right. This drainage wraps around Bryant and takes you to a tarn, from which the ascent is made. Hike up the tributary on the creek bed or on the trails alongside it. Stay left at all intersections. At GR412423 (marked with two large cairns and flagging on the left side of the creek), the trail ascends the steep left bank and then wanders through light forest before emerging on the open slopes of Bryant's northwest side. Continue traversing the slopes, eventually arriving at the clear and colourful waters of an unnamed tarn, referred to by some as Bryant Lake, for obvious reasons. Allow 2.5 hours to this point.

The remainder of the ascent is a less than inspiring slog up scree slopes on the east side of the tarn. Walk around the left side of the tarn for 100 m and turn left, aiming for the only rock band that stands in your way. Either go around the left side of the band or tackle it head-on to enjoy a few moves of hands-on scrambling. Unfortunately, the scrambling is over before it has begun and then it's loose scree and rubble all the way to the top—500 vertical m of it! The bright side is that higher up, with each step, the view starts to open up and suddenly an ocean of familiar peaks stands before you (actually behind you).

If you arrive at the summit to cloudy skies, you may start to wonder what prompted you to undertake this trip. If the skies are clear, enjoy a wonderful, peak-filled panorama. A fresh sprinkling of snow all around adds to the scenery dramatically.

Returning the same way is fine, but traversing over to the east summit and then down the east ridge makes for a very satisfying loop route and allows

The east ridge descent route. C scenic cliff bands. P parking area.
M Moose Mountain.

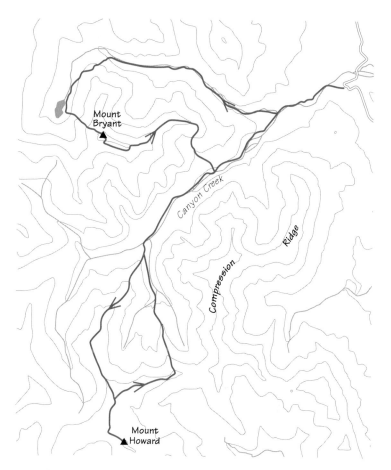

you to explore more of this interesting peak. Continue along the ridge heading east. There are a couple of narrow and mildly exposed sections. After ascending a wide ramp, the terrain suddenly becomes more serious. Here, either continue along the ridge, carefully downclimbing the exposed ridge, or downclimb to scree slopes on the right (easier, but still requiring care).

Unfortunately, regaining the ridge at this point quickly leads to more steep terrain that will require a rope. Instead, descend a scree gully on the south side of the mountain until you can take a sharp left, traversing below vertical walls of rock on wide, scree-covered ledges. Continue below the cliffs, but stay high. Circle around the impressive summit block and then gain the summit easily.

There are numerous descent options on the south side of the mountain from this summit, but the best one (though not the shortest) follows the east/northeast ridge most of the way. Head down the ridge, circumventing steeper sections or drop-offs on the right side. Stay on the ridge as much as possible. You're aiming for the very obvious reddish brown scree slopes that lead south to Canyon Creek. Once you hit the brown scree, continue almost to the end of it and then turn right and bomb down the scree, losing elevation at a tremendous rate. The scree soon runs out, but the terrain is still easy and enjoyable to descend. Aim for the drainage in the middle, but do not go into it. The last stunning piece of scenery will soon appear to your left in the form of an enormous cliff band. After a quick visit, continue down, again on the left side of the drainage. Arrive back down at Canyon Creek, turn left and follow the creek for about 2.5 km back to your vehicle.

Mount Howard 2,777 m

Difficulty Easy via north ridge
Round-trip time 8–10 hours
Elevation gain 1,040 m; more if you visit all the high points
Maps 82 J/15 Bragg Creek, Gem Trek Canmore and Bragg Creek

Mount Howard is an easy ascent from the north and a good late-season objective. The north ridge allows you to gain elevation quickly and then enjoy a terrific ridgewalk to the summit. Inaccessible from December 1 to May 15. Try from June on. Summit at GR419350.

Drive west on Highway 66 to the point where it becomes the Powderface Trail. Continue for 14.5 km and park in an open area where wide Canyon Creek meets the road (GR458419). Hike southwest up Canyon Creek, passing Compression Ridge on your left and Mount Bryant on your right. At a leisurely pace, you'll reach the start of Howard's north ridge in about 1.25–1.5 hours, beginning at GR422388 (see photo on p. 163). The ridge rises immediately from the left side of Canyon Creek, gaining elevation through light forest. The terrain soon opens up and you'll arrive at the first of many high points along this scenic ridge.

You really can't go wrong once on the ridge. Follow it as it trends southwest over a couple of high points and first turns southeast, then south, and finally southeast to the summit. Staying on the ridge throughout and visiting every high point provides the best scenery and views, even though it entails more elevation gain and the requisite losses. Save the side-sloping for the descent.

The north ridge ascent route, seen from Mount Bryant. S summit. G Mount Glasgow. AD alternate descent.

Start of the north ridge from Canyon Creek.

The upper ridge. S summit.

The ridge is fairly long. Expect to take 4–5 hours from car to summit. Though higher than Mount Bryant to the north, the summit view from Howard is not as far-reaching. Nevertheless, it is nothing to sneeze at and includes great views toward the Twins (Mounts Remus and Romulus), Glasgow, Fisher Peak, and The Wedge, to name a few.

For the descent, start by **returning** the same way. When you reach the high point north of the summit, either descend scree slopes into the valley and drainage to the northeast (the fastest route) or start heading east along the ridge that connects Howard to Compression Ridge. When you reach the last rib (ridge) before Compression Ridge (GR428363), turn left and descend the rib easily all the way to the valley bottom. This option allows you to stay high up and enjoy a little more of the beautiful surroundings. Both routes join up at a drainage that leads you back to Canyon Creek.

For those who have not completed the very enjoyable traverse of Compression Ridge, here's your chance to complete a long-loop route and get two summits in one trip. Continue east along the connecting ridge to Compression Ridge. Alan Kane's *Scrambles in the Canadian Rockies* contains an excellent detailed description. Note: Compression Ridge is a difficult scramble and far more involved than the easy ascent of Mount Howard.

Threepoint Mountain 2,595 m

Difficulty Easy/moderate via west slopes and northwest ridge
Round-trip time 9–13 hours
Elevation gain 1,000 m
Maps 82 J/10 Mount Rae, 82 J/15 Bragg Creek, Gem Trek Bragg Creek

Visiting the three high points of Threepoint Mountain is a surprisingly enjoyable trip with lots of scenic ridgewalking. A bike approach saves time and an alternate descent route makes for a pleasant loop route. A terrific late-season outing. Inaccessible from December 1 to May 15. Try from June on. Summit at GR534194.

The west side of Threepoint Mountain, seen from Cougar Mountain.

Drive west on Highway 66 and turn left into the Elbow Recreation area. Park at the second Trailhead Parking area across from the big suspension bridge. Sometimes this road is closed, in which case park at the first Trailhead Parking area and hike west alongside the Elbow River a few hundred metres to the bridge. Cross the bridge and hike or bike (preferable) the Big Elbow Trail for 8.3 km to the Big Elbow Campground. Continue along Big Elbow Trail for another 1 km or so, looking for a small drainage that comes down from the right (GR509207). This is where you'll want to head east to the Elbow River and find a place to cross.

Either boulder-hop or ford the river and continue east through the trees,

The ascent route, from the Elbow River.

toward the right side of the west-facing ascent slopes (see photo above). Pretty much any line of ascent will do here, but quickly you'll arrive at a rock band of crumbling shale. Ascend the band through one of numerous weaknesses and continue up to a second and more vertical band. This one may require some route-finding to circumvent and a few steps of moderate scrambling. Traverse right for easier terrain.

Above the second band, a quick stint through trees followed by a longish scree slog leads easily to the ridge. Aim for the left side of the very prominent buttress at the top. This slope gets fairly steep higher up and would not be safe when the avalanche danger is above a rating of "low." Fortunately, its west-facing orientation means that it will frequently get wind-blown free of snow.

At the impressive buttress, hike around to the left and then scramble up steeper rock to gain the ridge. An easier and faster (but less interesting route) traverses well below the ridge. Gain the ridge after circumventing the first major section. Once on the ridge, the route is straightforward, easy, and scenic. Follow the ridge to the first of Threepoint's three high points and then continue south over the second and finally to the true summit at an elevation of 2,595 m. Stay on the ridge throughout.

Needless to say, Threepoint is dwarfed by its neighbours to the west and south, but the view is satisfying nonetheless. Mount Rose is the slightly lower mountain connected to Threepoint. Unfortunately, a vertical rock band below the south-facing slopes of Threepoint render a direct traverse to Rose impossible. Farther south, Bluerock Mountain and Mount Burns dominate the view. A route to Bluerock's summit is described in *Gillean Daffern's Kananaskis Country Trail Guide, Volume 2*. Three Alan Kane scrambles from *Scrambling in the Canadian Rockies* (Cougar, Banded, and Glasgow) line the southwest and west horizon.

The most enjoyable way off the mountain is the west ridge, though **returning** the way you came does not present any difficulties. If snow remains on the west ridge, an ice axe, crampons, and even a rope may be necessary. There are a couple of sections where the ridge is narrow, and slipping down snow slopes on either side would have serious consequences. If the ridge is snow-free, it is a pleasant and easy hike. Simply follow the ridge down, taking the ridge on the right when it splits (see photo below). One small rock band interrupts the ridge and can be carefully downclimbed head-on or circumvented on the left side.

Much lower down, stay near the edge as the ridge starts to curve left, with an increasingly steep drop-off on your right. Hike through light forest down to the creek far below. Follow the creek out (easier above the bank on the right side) as it joins up with the Elbow River. Ford the river and continue west to find Big Elbow Trail and the easy route back to your vehicle.

West Ridge descent route.

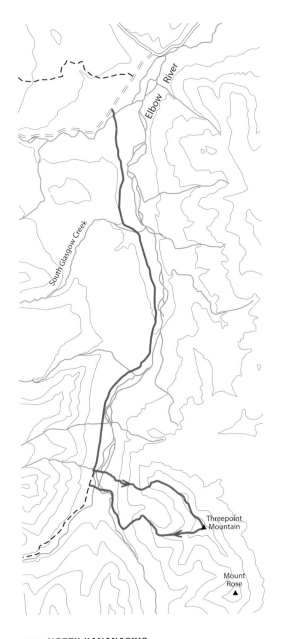

Elbow River

South Glasgow Creek

Threepoint
Mountain

Mount
Rose

Good scrambling on Ribbon Peak.

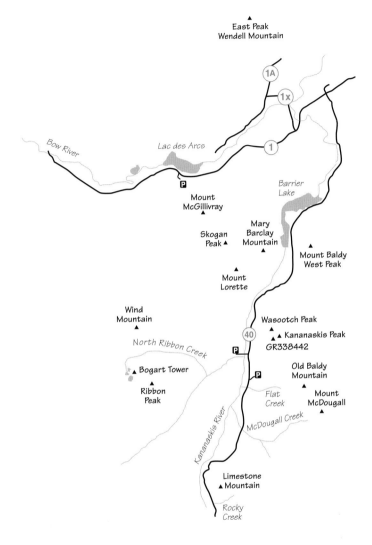

East Peak
Wendell Mountain

1A

1x

Bow River

Lac des Arcs

1

Barrier
Lake

P

Mount
McGillivray

Mary
Barclay
Mountain

Skogan
Peak

Mount Baldy
West Peak

Mount
Lorette

Wind
Mountain

Wasootch Peak

40

Kananaskis Peak

GR338442

North Ribbon Creek

P

Old Baldy
Mountain

Bogart Tower

P

Flat
Creek

Mount
McDougall

Ribbon
Peak

Kananaskis River

McDougall Creek

Limestone
Mountain

Rocky
Creek

The peaks in this section are definitely your best bet for year-round scrambling. Of course, any winter attempt at one of these peaks is dependent upon having "no" or "low" avalanche potential and crampons, and an ice axe may be necessary. Approaches are generally short, which makes them ideal for the shorter days of the winter months. Wind Mountain and Ribbon Peak are the exceptions here, as they both have long approaches that would be extremely arduous in deep snow. Naturally, all the peaks in this section also make great summer objectives.

East Peak of Wendell Mountain 2,294 m

Difficulty Easy via south ridge; difficult via col and west ridge
Round-trip time 6–8 hours
Elevation gain 1,200 m
Maps 82 O/3 Canmore

Many climbers will be quite familiar with this peak, as it is home to numerous rock routes. Fortunately for those without a technical background, there is an easy scramble route to the summit. To best enjoy the terrific rock scenery this trip has to offer, the "scenic" route is recommended. The "direct" route is ideal for the return trip. A far more challenging ascent route also exists and can be combined with the south ridge to complete a loop. Try from May on.

East peak from the east ridge of Mount Yamnuska. SR scenic route. DR direct route. S summit.

From the 1X/1A intersection, drive 2 km east and turn left onto a gravel road that leads quickly to the Yamnuska parking lot. Starting at the far end of the parking lot, hike the trail as it crosses the maintenance road and then winds its way slowly up the hillside. At the sign, turn right and follow the hiker's trail until it reaches the east ridge of Mount Yamnuska (about 1 hour). Decide which route you want to take, the scenic route or the direct route.

If you choose the former, upon reaching the ridge, look for a clear spot to the right where you can see the objective to the northwest. Head downhill directly to the right side of the mountain. At the low point, continue uphill to the base of the stunning vertical walls of rock. Turn left and start a lengthy but thoroughly enjoyable traverse of the mountain's south face on a good scree trail.

If you choose the direct route, upon reaching the ridge, continue heading west on the trail, looking through the trees for open slopes to your right. Once out in the open, descend grassy slopes heading directly for the west side of the objective.

Both routes join up at the west side of the east peak. Ascend scree slopes on the south ridge. Slabs to the right provide some relief from the scree. The route looks tricky and guarded by steep rock bands, however, such is not the case and the scrambling should never be difficult. Route-find your way through the upper rock bands (trending left as necessary) and gain the upper

The south ridge of the east peak.

south ridge. Turn left and hike easily to the summit. After taking in the beautiful contrast of rugged peaks to the west and flat prairies to the east, **return** the same way. **Do not** attempt to downclimb the west ridge and return via the "difficult" route. The downclimb is very steep and exposed, and route-finding will be extremely tricky throughout.

Another, but difficult, route to the summit is via the col and west ridge. This is a terrific route that, when combined with the easy descent via the south ridge, provides the most comprehensive experience of this interesting peak and outstanding area. Gain the west side of the peak via the "scenic" or "direct" route. Instead of going up the south ridge, traverse the west side of the mountain on an obvious scree trail. Eventually this trail ends as the steep walls of Wendell Mountain rear up to block the way. Look for the path of least resistance to the right, evident through a maze of rock bands and gullies. Moderate scrambling with a little route-finding will take you in short order to a scree slope that goes all the way to the col of Wendell Mountain and its east peak. As you make your way through the gullies and up the scree slopes, make sure to look back at your ascent route, as it will appear quite different if you choose to return via this route.

At the col, turn right and follow the west ridge to the summit. The first pinnacle is obviously circumvented on the right side. After that, stay on the ridge until you arrive at steeper terrain that again must be circumvented. Lose

Difficult route from the west side of the east peak. C Wendell/east peak col.

Summit block from the west ridge of the east peak. C crux. S summit.

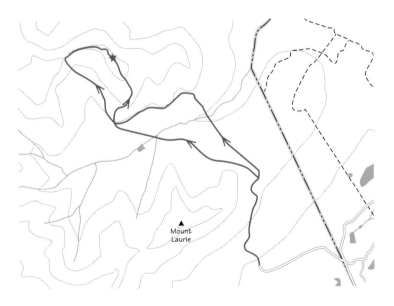

elevation on the right, traverse south a little, and then look for a way back to the ridge on the left side of the summit block. Choose your route carefully, as you may have to retreat this way if the crux is not to your liking. Back on the ridge you are now confronted with the crux. Scramble very carefully up the steep and then narrow ridge. The rock is loose, so check all hand- and foot-holds carefully. If snow remains on any part of the ridge, a rope and climbing protection may be necessary—a slip down either side of the ridge would be fatal. Either **return** the same way (provided you feel comfortable downclimbing the crux) or descend the easy south ridge (do south ridge route in reverse).

Mount McGillivray 2,450 m

Difficulty Difficult via west side
Round-trip time 8–11 hours
Elevation gain 1,200 m
Maps 82 O/3 Canmore, Gem Trek Canmore

Lying immediately west of popular Heart Mountain, Mount McGillivray is a familiar peak when seen from the Trans-Canada Highway. Its prominent and distinctive north buttress is the key to this ascent. As a front-range peak, McGillivray can be snow-free quite early in the season, however, snow lining the exposed and narrow upper ridge can put a quick stop to a summit bid. Try from mid-May on.

Park at a small parking lot on the south side of the Trans-Canada, 3.4 km east of the Dead Man's Flats turnoff. Hike the old road for several hundred metres looking a little to the left for the "hump" that starts the ascent. Turn left onto the Trans-Canada Trail, arriving at a clearing on your right in a few minutes. Turn right, aiming for the treed hump in front and to the left of the visible and steep rock face. Initially, the slope is steep but eases soon after. Heading southeast, a long and gradual ascent through the trees follows. As long as you are going up, you can't go wrong.

Eventually, the terrain opens up and the north buttress becomes visible. Simply aim for the base of this buttress, climbing up open, shaley scree slopes through another stint of tress, and then onto more scree. Allow 1.5–2 hours to get to this point. It is not necessary to ascend all the way to the base of the buttress. When feasible, start side-sloping the scree bowl on the right (west) side of the north buttress toward a break in the far side. When far enough over, it is possible to scramble directly to the ridge, however, the rock is very loose, and the use of caution is recommended. Probably better to simply go all the way to the far end, where only easy to moderate scrambling is involved.

Approaching the north buttress.

The two routes to the ridge, along the second bowl. D difficult route. E easy route. S summit.

Upon reaching the far end, decide whether you want to take the easy route to the summit ridge or the difficult one. Unless you are familiar with the easy route, it will be hard to find the easy way down if you take the difficult way up, so make sure you are comfortable downclimbing what you will upclimb via the difficult route. Regardless of which route you take, both will join up for the final push to the summit, which is narrow and exposed and therefore rated difficult.

To follow the easy route to the summit ridge, continue traversing west, below cliff bands of the second bowl, until an easy route to your left becomes visible. Turn left and ascend scree slopes, taking the path of least resistance. The route neatly works its way above a significant cliff band to the right. As you ascend, take careful note of the route and look back frequently to see how it looks from above—on descent, the route can be difficult to see. Once above the cliff band, the summit is visible to the right. Head directly for the summit ridge or up and to the right for a more direct line.

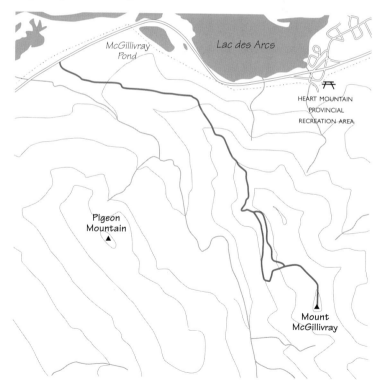

The difficult route to the summit ridge traverses a scree ledge between the two cliff bands of the second bowl. The crux is getting up to the ledge. Once around the south side of the first bowl, turn left and hike east to the base of the buttress. Scramble up an obvious, steep gully and then traverse right to gain the ledge. Traverse the ledge along the base of the upper rock band, until you reach the end, where the rock band starts to break down. Look for a place to scramble up—some difficult scrambling here. Gain the upper slopes and head up to the ridge.

After gaining the ridge via either route, follow it toward the summit. Take extra care on the narrow and exposed final 50 m. Enjoy the front-row view of the four peaks of Mount Lougheed and Collembola before **returning** the same way you came up. Again, trying to find the easy route down may prove to be arduous and time-consuming if you took the difficult one up.

Mount Baldy via West Ridge 2,192 m

Difficulty Difficult and exposed; a climber's scramble (approach
    shoes recommended)
Round–trip time 4.5–6 hours
Elevation gain 825 m
Maps 82 J/14 Spray Lakes Reservoir, 82 O/3 Canmore, Gem Trek Canmore

If you've done Mount Baldy by the normal route, or you're looking for a shorter and more challenging route to Baldy's west summit, you're in luck. The west ridge offers a short approach with difficult and interesting scrambling and some fairly intense exposure. This route must be snow and ice free. Try from mid-May on.

Drive 14.4 km south on Highway 40 and park on the side of the road by an obvious rubble-filled drainage (about 300 m south of O'Shaughnessy Falls). Although it is feasible to ascend treed slopes directly below the ridge, a well-worn trail farther south runs along the left side of the drainage and takes all the guess work out of the first section. Follow this trail to tree line. If you really want to get your money's worth on the trip, ascend the actual drainage from the road, enjoying interesting scenery and moderate scrambling up a variety of good quality rock. When the canyon gets too difficult, find an escape route by ascending steep slopes on the left to gain the west ridge. Follow the ridge to tree line.

When the scrambling begins, the most exciting route follows the ridge throughout, though the first section circles to the left around a very steep slab. Often the ridge may appear to lead to steep drop-offs, but this is a façade and easier terrain waits at the top of each section. The crux is a very steep-looking

The west ridge of Baldy's west peak, seen from Heart Mountain. S summit.

The ascent route from Highway 40. D drainage. S summit. SD south ridge descent route.

Mark approaches the crux.

A close-up of the crux.

and narrow section that, again, appears to lead to a drop-off. This is not the case. Scramble carefully up the centre of the very exposed ridge onto a small plateau. A shorter, less steep section follows, but still, a slip anywhere on the crux section would most likely be fatal. If the crux is not to your liking, downclimb to scree on the right side of the ridge just before the crux, and then continue up scree or slabs to avoid the crux. After the crux, more enjoyable (and easier) scrambling leads to the summit ridge and then a pleasant stroll to the top.

Several options exist for descent. Avoid the tempting west-facing slopes immediately south of the ascent route. This terrain is steep, rubbly, and

requires much route-finding and detouring around steep drop-offs. Instead choose one of three options.

I most recommend the following (easiest) route. Take the south and then southwest ridge of Baldy's west peak. From the summit, continue south down the ridge on a noticeable trail. The most exciting route stays on the sometimes airy ridge crest throughout, however, a few mildly exposed sections can be avoided by dropping down to scree slopes to the right if you're not in the mood. Just before a multi-cairned high point of the south ridge, the ridge narrows considerably. If up for a little challenge (be ready for some serious exposure on the left side!), ascend a short but steep rock-step and then traverse the very narrow ridge—all but the most courageous and sure of balance will probably choose to bum-shuffle across this short section.

At the high point, trend right on a trail down toward the treed bump of the southwest ridge. Once past the rock outcrops, follow the treed ridge for about 15 minutes and then either turn left and descend slopes toward Baldy Pass Trail, or turn right and descend slightly steeper slopes directly to the highway. If you go left, upon reaching the trail, turn right, follow it out to the road and then turn right again and walk along the highway for about 1 km to your vehicle. The route to the right of the ridge is shorter, but it is steeper at the top and is not that much faster.

The second route down is more difficult. Use Alan Kane's route in reverse. Carefully downclimb the east face of the west peak and then continue down to the col between the west and south peaks. Turn left, descend scree slopes (possible glissade if there's enough snow) and follow the drainage out to the highway, about 1 km north of your car.

The third possible route is the most difficult. Return the way you came. If at all uneasy about downclimbing what you have upclimbed, use one of the other alternate routes. Downclimbing the crux presents a considerable challenge and is not recommended.

Mary Barclay's Mountain 2,250 m

Difficulty Moderate via south ridge, with mild exposure near the top
Round-trip time 4.5–6 hours
Elevation gain 850 m
Maps 82 J/14 Spray Lakes Reservoir, 82 O/3 Canmore, Gem Trek Canmore

Provided the Kananaskis River is low enough to ford, the south ridge of unofficial Mary Barclay's Mountain is a scenic and interesting scramble. This trip makes for a great early-season warm-up. Try from May on.

The ascent and descent routes, seen from near Highway 40. KR Kananaskis River. S summit.

Drive 17.9 km south on Highway 40 and park at the pull-off on the east side of the road right after the Wasootch Creek Bridge. Check out the ascent route as you hike along the mostly dried-up creek bed to the Kananaskis River. The objective is to gain the south ridge as soon as possible. Wade the river, provided it is low enough to do so. If not, pick another trip or see the Mount Lorette description to find out how to circumvent the river crossing. After crossing the river, scramble up the steep embankment on the other side and hike through light forest to the start of the south ridge.

Follow the ridge in its entirety to the summit. Near the top, the ridge gets steeper and narrows for a short section; use care on this mildly exposed terrain. The summit panorama is quite respectable, highlighting many familiar scrambles and other peaks.

For your descent, **return** the same way, or, for a little variety, continue heading down the northwest ridge to a col and then left down easy slopes to the drainage. Follow the drainage out to the river.

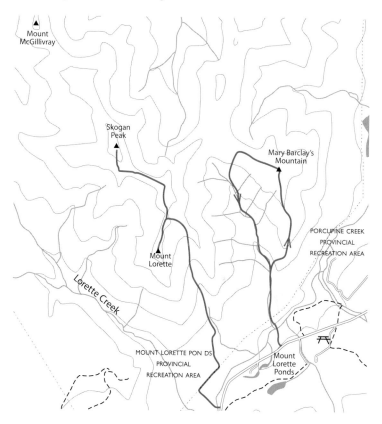

Mount Lorette 2,487 m

Difficulty Moderate via south gully and northeast ridge
Round-trip time 6–8 hours
Elevation gain 1,100 m
Maps 82 J/14 Spray Lakes Reservoir, Gem Trek Canmore

The normal route up Mount Lorette is an airy and exposed 5.4-km climb via the south ridge. Although climbers sometimes do this route without a rope, several deaths have occurred and it is therefore not recommended as a scramble. For experienced hikers and scramblers, the climber's descent route offers a much safer and easier route to the summit. Although little more than a steep hike, the scenery and summit view are enough to make this a worthwhile excursion. As well, the trip can be extended to a higher and unnamed peak to the north ("Skogan Peak") for a long but very rewarding day. Try from mid-May on.

The ascent route, from Highway 40. H first high point. S summit. KR Kananaskis River.

Park on the west side of Highway 40, 19.4 km south of the Trans-Canada. From here, the initial part of the ascent route is very obvious and should be noted. Wade the frigid Kananaskis River, provided it is low enough to do so. If not, pick another trip or continue driving south on Highway 40 and turn right at the Kananaskis Village turnoff. About 1 km along the road take your first right to a parking area. Hike or bike the Stoney Trail, heading north, for approximately 5 km. The ascent route will quickly become visible and obvious.

Back to the river crossing: once across, head west through light forest, eventually arriving at the wide-open Stoney Trail, where you will be able to clearly see the ascent gully (make note of this gully, in case you lose the trail). Hike north along the trail until you arrive at the top of a steep embankment. Turn left and continue on another trail that parallels the drainage. In short time, it is possible to head left through light forest to the ascent drainage or continue north until you reach the point where the drainage crosses Stoney Trail. Turn left up the drainage and look for the trail that runs along its left side. It will take you, without difficulty, all the way to a col that leads to the summit of Lorette (stay to the right when the grade becomes steeper before the col). Be patient—this gully is fairly foreshortened.

At the col, turn left (west) and make your way to a minor summit, where you will be able to view the remainder of the route and another route toward the highest peak of the range—"Skogan Peak" at GR302516. At the high point, continue heading in a westerly direction and follow the ridge easily to the summit. The ridge is mildly exposed in a couple of sections, but these can be avoided on the right if necessary. On the way, the impressive, vertical east face of Lorette and higher unnamed peak to the north should be enough to keep you interested. After enjoying a very pleasant summit panorama, **return** the same way. Back at the first high point, there is the option to continue on to "Skogan Peak" to the north (see the next trip).

"Skogan Peak" at GR302516 2,662 m

Difficulty Moderate via southeast ridge; exposure
Round-trip time 9–11 hours
Elevation gain 1,250 m
Maps 82 J/14 Spray Lakes Reservoir, 82 O/3 Canmore, Gem Trek Canmore

This is the highest point of the Lorette/McGillivray traverse, surpassing both mountains in height by a fair margin. It is also a terrific scramble. Though the scrambling is never too difficult, it is fairly exposed in places. Any snow remaining on the ridge would add considerable danger and push the ascent into the realm of mountaineering. Try from June on.

See the route description for Mount Lorette above and follow it up to the first high point. Continue north along the easy ridge, down and then up to the next high point. Here, the connecting ridge to the summit will be more clearly visible for assessment. Again, if snow remains on the ridge, this may be the end of the line. If not, start along the ridge. It soon narrows and becomes exposed on both sides. The first section of exposed scrambling can be

The ascent route, as seen from the first high point. DS double summit.

The ridge and upper slopes. B bypass of the first narrow section. FS false summit. TS true summit.

avoided by dropping down to the left and traversing below it. Return to the ridge and continue on until the next narrow section. This one cannot be circumvented unless you lose a great amount of elevation. The best strategy for this section is to traverse on small ledges on the left side of the ridge, just below it. This serves a dual purpose as it will prevent you from seeing the butt-clenching drop on the right side!

Once across, scramble up the steeper rock face near the ridge and continue for a short while. Angled bands of rock now line the ridge, preventing farther access along it. Start traversing left, going across successive gullies until the summit (actually a false summit) is in view. Be prepared for a few short but necessary elevation losses. Do not regain the ridge too early—you may be forced to retreat. When the false summit is visible, scramble up slabs and/or scree toward it.

At the false summit, descend to a col between it and the true summit and then continue easily up to the top. As the highest point of the massif, the summit provides a wonderful view. Looking down on Lorette to the south and McGillivray to the north should make you feel good about completing this trip, the longest and perhaps most challenging of the three. **Return** the same way. Tagging Mount Lorette on return will add about 1.5–2 hours and approximately 100 m of elevation but will save you another ford of the Kananaskis River and the long trudge up the ascent gully.

"Wasootch Peak" at GR334455 2,352 m

Difficulty Easy
Round-trip time 3.5–5 hours
Elevation gain 900 m
Maps 82 J/14 Spray Lakes Reservoir, Gem Trek Canmore

There are at least four distinct routes to the summit of unofficially named "Wasootch Peak:" two from the Wasootch Creek side and two from the Highway 40 side. The route described below is the easiest one to the summit and best combined with an ascent of Kananaskis Peak at GR345444. While "Wasootch Peak" is mostly a steep hike, GR345444 is a considerably more challenging undertaking, requiring steep and exposed scrambling.

Start at the dried-up creek bed just north of the Kananaskis Village turnoff, 23.3 km south of the Trans-Canada. Park on the shoulder of the east side of the road. Stick to the left side of the creek bed, eventually finding and following an excellent trail that leads pretty much to the summit via the south ridge. Take an easy line up scree slopes or explore the rock for a little hands-on

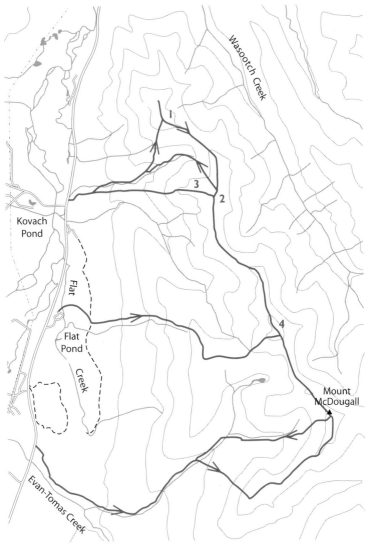

1: Wasootch Peak; 2: Kananaskis Peak; 3: GR338442; 4: Old Baldy Mountain.

The route to the south summit of "Wasootch Peak" from Highway 40. NS north summit. SS south summit.

scrambling. Enjoy the pleasant view and then decide where you want to go next. If home, **return** the same way. You can extend the trip slightly by following the ridge to the north to a slightly lower summit at GR334455: Given its close proximity, it is worth the minimal effort. A more serious and rewarding extension exists by heading south to Kananaskis Peak at GR345444 (see next trip).

"Kananaskis Peak" at GR345444 2,419 m

Difficulty "Wasootch Peak" Easy; GR345444: Difficult, with some exposure
Round-trip time 7–11 hours
Elevation gain 1,290 m
Maps 82 J/14 Spray Lakes Reservoir, Gem Trek Canmore

Lying immediately south of "Wasootch Peak," "Kananaskis Peak" does not appear to be a significant summit when seen from the road. It is, however, the highest point of the north end of the Mount McDougall massif and has a beautifully scenic ridgewalk. An alternate descent route offers a very easy way off the mountain. Try from mid-May on.

Ascent and descent routes from "Wasootch Peak." S summit. D descent route. ED easy descent route.

Follow the directions to the summit of "Wasootch Peak" (previous trip).

From the summit of Wasootch Peak, downclimb a short section to where a small rock outcrop blocks the route. Climb up and over the outcrop (there is some exposure, so use care) continue down to the low point, and then up. The route is obvious. The crux follows shortly after. Upon arriving at a steep rock band that guards the upper slopes, trend right to find a weakness where

The crux.

the rock is the least steep. Even here, the rock is loose, downsloping, and steep. If the scrambling exceeds your comfort level, turn back. Also, consider that you must downclimb this section if you fail to reach the summit.

Continue up easier terrain, taking the path of least resistance. At one point, you will come to another outcrop barring the route. Circumvent this obstacle on the left side. The first summit follows shortly. Perhaps the most enjoyable section is the traverse from the first summit to the highest point of the trip at GR345444. Stay on the ridge throughout and enjoy the beautiful scenery of slabby, vertical rock on your right. There are a couple of exposed sections that you may want to bum-shuffle over. Expect approximately 30 minutes for the traverse.

At the summit, look back to see the long route you have just completed and get ready for a much easier descent. Continue heading north along the ridge (including one short, mildly exposed section) and then drop down to a small col on the right. From that point, scree-surf down the easy, north-facing slopes. At the bottom, follow the creek right back to your car.

GR338442 2,283 m

Difficulty Easy to moderate via west slopes
Round-trip time 6–10 hours
Elevation gain 830 m
Maps 82 J/14 Spray Lakes Reservoir, Gem Trek Canmore

An easy trip that won't get you to a significant summit but does offer magnificent rock scenery and the option to continue on to Kananaskis Peak at GR345444, where a loop route is possible. A good early-season trip to get you back in shape. In warm years, the ascent may be possible from mid-April on.

The ascent route from Highway 40.

Start at the Highway 40 sign just north of the Kananaskis Village turnoff at a dried creek bed (GR316442). The peak is directly east—head straight for it. The bushwhacking ranges from moderate to downright nasty—persist, the effort will be worth it. A compass or GPS may be useful.

Once above tree line (approximately 1 hour), you are rewarded with the terrific and somewhat intimidating views of the peak's huge and near-vertical walls. Not to worry—you won't have to climb any. Continue up to the first rock outcrop and go around it to the left. The route is quite obvious. With the exception of a short, steeper section right before the summit, the scrambling should never be too difficult. If you have the time, take the opportunity to explore some of the fascinating terrain on your way up (or down).

Just before the summit, the terrain becomes a little steeper, but it never demands more than moderate scrambling. After enjoying the summit panorama, **return** the same way, or continue heading east toward Kananaskis Peak. This traverse requires a little more route-finding and scrambling than the ascent to GR338442, but it is enjoyable and quite easy. For the most part, it is possible to stay on the ridge. One steeper rock band about halfway across can be circumvented on the right, though this does require some elevation loss. The final push to the summit of GR345444 requires you to descend a little to a brown scree col and then follow the ridge as it curves up and to the left. The summit of GR345444 is only a few minutes away, but the ridge does narrow significantly right before the top.

The brown scree is also the key to the alternate descent and loop route. **Return** to the col and start down the scree slopes in a northerly direction. The scree is great for surfing, and you should be able to lose a significant amount of elevation in a very short time. Once at the bottom, follow the creek back to your vehicle.

"Old Baldy Mountain" at GR356417 2,728 m

Difficulty Easy/moderate via west ridge
Round-trip time 7–10 hours
Elevation gain 1,280 m
Maps 82 J/14 Spray Lakes Reservoir, Gem Trek Canmore

As the highest point of the massif, one would think this peak deserves an official name. Such is not the case (at the time of writing anyway!). Don't let this stop you from enjoying this easy and very scenic ascent. Problems are few and even if you don't make it all the way to the summit, Old Baldy Ridge is a fine destination in itself. Try from June on.

There are two approaches to gain Old Baldy Ridge, where the ascent to the summit of Old Baldy Mountain starts.

For option one, which is longer, park at the Evan-Thomas parking lot on Highway 40, 28 km south of the Trans-Canada Highway. Hike the Evan Thomas Trail for approximately 1.8 km (take a left at the "Trail not maintained …" sign). Several hundred metres after the sign, look for a small cairn on the left side of the trail, just before a drainage crosses the trail. Take a left onto the trail by the cairn (Old Baldy Trail—unsigned). Follow this trail as it parallels McDougall Creek for approximately 4.5 km, heading northeast and then north. Soon after, the trail starts to curve east. Leave the trail here and continue north up easy slopes to the col between Old Baldy Ridge (left) and your objective (right).

For the second approach to the ridge, the shorter option, park at Boundary Ranch, 25.8 km south of the Trans-Canada on Highway 40. Hike along the dirt road (horse trail) heading east until it curves south and eventually runs into Flat Creek. Turn left and follow the trail that parallels the creek on its north side. This takes you up steep, treed slopes to the wonderful viewpoint of Old Baldy Ridge. From here, you can see the remainder of the west ridge leading to the summit of Old Baldy Mountain.

The west ridge seen from Old Baldy Ridge.

From Old Baldy ridge or the col, the route up Old Baldy Mountain is as easy and obvious as it looks. Gain the west ridge and stay on it until you get to the summit. Staying on or near the edge of the ridge offers the most scenic views, especially an impressive near-vertical slab about a third of the way up. Though initially steep, the grade eases in short time, providing an easy and enjoyable ascent to the top.

The summit offers a splendid panorama in all directions. Of special note are the ridgewalks heading both north and south from the summit. If you are looking to nab the two highest peaks of the range, head south to Mount McDougall, again staying on the ridge throughout. It will take about 1 hour to get to McDougall's summit (see Mount McDougall description for descents off this peak). For the descent from Old Baldy Mountain, **return** the same way.

Mount McDougall 2,726 m

Difficulty Moderate/difficult via southwest ridge
Round-trip time 7–11 hours
Elevation gain 1,200 m
Maps 82 J/14 Spray Lakes Reservoir, Gem Trek Canmore

Mount McDougall is the only official peak of this massif, but still sees very few visitors. The fairly lengthy approach and tedious slog to the ridge may have something to do with this. Once above the tree line, however, the southwest ridge offers an interesting and enjoyable route to the summit. If snow remains on the route, an ice axe and crampons may be needed. Try from June on.

McDougall from Highway 40. VP "Volcano Peak." S summit.

Park at the Evan-Thomas parking lot on Highway 40, 28 km south of the Trans-Canada Highway. Hike the Evan Thomas Trail for approximately 1.8 km (take a left at the "Trail not maintained …" sign). Several hundred metres after the sign, look for a small cairn on the left side of the trail, just before a drain-age crosses the trail. Take a left on the trail by the cairn—this is the unsigned Old Baldy Trail. Follow the trail through light forest for approximately 30 minutes as it parallels McDougall Creek. The ascent route is now to your right—look for an open avalanche slope. At GR337388 (approx.), cross McDougall Creek and start up easy slopes, heading for the

The upper slopes from just beyond "Volcano Peak." S summit. D suggested descent route.

open area. Look for a boulder field. Ascend these tedious and foreshortened slopes to the ridge and turn left, toward the volcano-shaped, western outlier of McDougall. It is not necessary to ascend this outlier, but it does give you an excellent view of the remainder of the route and requires minimal effort. Besides, you may decide against completing the entire route and the outlier does a satisfying objective in itself. If you don't want to ascend the outlier, traverse around the peak on the south (right) side.

The summit of the outlier is a good place to take a break and survey of rest of the route, as well as enjoy views of the surrounding peaks. The ascent up McDougall is quite obvious from this vantage point, although unseen are several drop-offs and narrow sections that add a little excitement. Also, the true summit is the peak on the left. Descend easily to the col and then make your way along the crest of the ridge, taking care on several narrow and mildly exposed sections. Most of the exposure can be avoided by dropping down to the right side of the ridge and traversing below.

Soon you arrive at another low col where the ridge widens considerably. Slog up the ridge until, once again, it narrows and you arrive at a steep drop-off—the crux. Though only about 5 m in height, downclimbing this crux will probably be beyond the comfort level of most people. It is much safer to descend slopes to your left and downclimb through one of several weaknesses in the rock band. Regain the ridge and continue on. A similar situation occurs a little farther on, but is far less severe and downclimbing it should be manageable. If not, again drop down to the left and find an easier route.

The lower south summit is now only minutes away. An enjoyable ridgewalk leads easily to the true summit, farther north. If you have completed the Alan Kane scrambles in the area, the surrounding peaks should be very familiar. Mount Kidd dominates to the west, with Bogart and Sparrowhawk beyond. Also clearly visible are The Tower, Galatea, Gusty, and The Fortress. Immediately north is the slightly higher Old Baldy Mountain at GR356417.

There are several options for descent. You could return the same way, but the easiest descent is to head down west-facing slopes directly below the summit. Trend left, aiming for the gully in the centre of the slope. Initially the grade is quite gentle, but does get steeper lower down. At the bottom of the slope, follow McDougall Creek back to Old Baldy Trail. A third descent route would be to continue heading northwest down the ridge. This route is entirely visible from the summit and curves around to the west before dropping down to McDougall Creek and out. Along the way you will encounter a small but exposed step that must be carefully downclimbed.

The Big Traverse (Wasootch Peak to Mount McDougall) 2,728 m

Difficulty Difficult
Round-trip time 13–16 hours
Elevation gain 1,700 m
Maps 82 J/14 Spray Lakes Reservoir, Gem Trek Canmore

Instead of picking off the many high points of the Mount McDougall massif one or two at a time, as my brother and I did, it is possible to get them all in a single day trip. This is a very long and physically strenuous trip, requiring approximately 1,600 m of elevation gain and a tremendous amount of horizontal distance. As well, completing the entire circuit will leave you about 6 km from your car—two cars or a bike stashed at the other end will save you time and energy.

The traverse can be done in either direction, but north to south is preferable as most of the difficult sections will then be upclimbed, not downclimbed. A detailed description is pointless, as the ridge allows only one route. Basically, follow the route for "Wasootch Peak" and "Kananaskis Peak," then continue south along the ridge up to Old Baldy Mountain and then over to Mount McDougall. There are several exposed situations and you'll want snow-free conditions. If you decide to bail out somewhere along the line, the best bet is down the west ridge from Old Baldy Mountain, or descend west-facing slopes just before reaching the top of Old Baldy. This second option means you'll have to re-ascend the east side of Old Baldy Ridge, which probably defeats the purpose of bailing out!

Other suggested routes for the McDougall Range:
"Wasootch Peak" and "Kananaskis Peak"
GR338442 and "Kananaskis Peak"
Mount McDougall and Old Baldy Mountain

Wind Mountain 3,108 m

Difficulty Moderate via southwest slopes
Round-trip time 9–12 hours
Elevation gain 1,630 m
Maps 82 J/14 Spray Lakes Reservoir, Gem Trek Canmore

Often referred to as the fourth peak of Mount Lougheed, Wind Mountain has an almost identical elevation to the summit of Lougheed, and, like its northern brother, rewards those who can handle the long approach and 1,600+ m of elevation gain with a magnificent view. Try from July on. Summit at GR232462.

Note: The peak identified as Wind Mountain on the Gem-Trek map (2,819 m) is the lower eastern outlier of the mountain described here.

Take the Kananaskis Village turnoff, 23.4 km south of the Trans-Canada on Highway 40. Follow the signs for Ribbon Creek and park at the Upper Ribbon Creek parking lot. Hike or bike (recommended) the Ribbon Creek Trail for 3.4 km. Look for a cairn and good trail on the right side of the trail that marks the start of the Memorial Lakes Trail (GR272430). Turn right onto the trail, paralleling North Ribbon Creek. In about 1 hour, the trail suddenly becomes very steep as it ascends alongside a nearby waterfall. Near the top of this steep section, a side trail appears on your right. Take this right fork as it gains elevation on the hillside and then turns north up the valley high above a creek. The trail eventually peters out, but the route is obvious as you continue up the valley, with the imposing walls of Mount Sparrowhawk's east face to your left and the shapely form of Wind Mountain on the right.

Soon the terrain opens up and you have a decision to make: the direct route (moderately difficult) or the scenic route (difficult). Most will want to take the direct route. The scenic route offers more variety and a better view, as

The two routes up Wind as seen from the south ridge. S summit. DR direct route. SR scenic route.

well as more interesting, challenging, and exposed scrambling. It does, however, require a fairly big elevation loss and will likely add at least an hour to the overall trip time. This route also offers other potentially more challenging routes up the face, however, while the terrain may look straightforward, it is often deceptively steep and exposed, and is therefore not recommended.

For the direct route, continue up the valley, aiming for the scree slopes in the middle of the southwest face of Wind Mountain. Ascend the left side of the scree ramp and make your way up easy terrain, through the lower rock bands (moderate scrambling up one). Scenic and more significant rock bands soon rear up in front of you. Start angling right, following the line of scree toward the west ridge. Gain the west ridge and follow first a scree trail, then slabs to the summit.

For the scenic route, turn right (east) and make your way up to the south ridge of Wind Mountain. Follow the ridge, enjoying a few sections of scrambling on the way. When you arrive at a large and vertical rock band, (clearly not scrambling terrain) traverse around its right side to find a steep, exposed upclimb that angles slightly left. Ascend this step carefully and then continue along the ridge to the next rock band, which again would require technical climbing. At this point, you have to lose elevation on the left side of the band, down scree and steep slabs. There are numerous points along the way where it appears to be feasible to ascend the band to easier terrain, however these

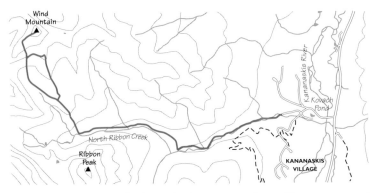

only lead to steep and difficult terrain that most people would want a rope and protection for. To play it safe, descend all the way down to the scree slopes that join up with the direct route and then follow that route up. After losing all this elevation, you may question why you bothered with this diversion in the first place, but at least you got some good scrambling in and saw a good deal more of the mountain.

Return down the direct route.

Ribbon Peak 2,880 m

Difficulty Difficult, exposed scrambling via south ridge
Round-trip time 9–13 hours
Elevation gain 1,400 m
Maps 82 J/14 Spray Lakes Reservoir, Gem Trek Canmore

Ribbon Peak lives figuratively and literally in the shadow of much taller Mount Bogart. The two peaks blend so well together, one might have to look twice to discern the outline of Ribbon Peak when seen from Highway 40. The south ridge involves a lengthy and considerably exposed knife-edge ridge traverse. Much of the exposure can be avoided, however this trip is included only for experienced scramblers. Snow may persist in the sheltered valley of the Memorial Lakes. Note: Ribbon Peak is actually the summit identified as Mount Bogart on NTS maps (see photo on p. 203). Try from mid-July on.

Take the Kananaskis Village turnoff, 23.4 km south of the Trans-Canada on Highway 40. Follow the signs for Ribbon Creek and park at the Upper Ribbon Creek parking lot. Hike or bike (recommended) the Ribbon Creek Trail for 3.4 km. Look for a cairn and a good trail on the right side of the trail that marks the start of the Memorial Lakes Trail (GR272430). Turn right onto the trail that soon parallels North Ribbon Creek. Hike the well-used trail 4.6 km, past the two lower Memorial Lakes and up to the third. Scope out Bogart's Tower looking down over the third lake as you pass by—you may want to run up it on the return trip.

From a scenic vantage point above the third lake, Mount Bogart dominates to the southwest and Ribbon Peak to the southeast. The first goal is to ascend the headwall. Traverse rubble slopes coming off Bogart toward the obvious rubble/scree slope at the end of the valley. Once on this slope, you'll

Ribbon Peak from above the Third Memorial Lake. S summit.

find the terrain to be steep and very unstable—be careful. At the top, work your way left onto a wide, downsloping scree ledge and continue traversing left. There are many locations to overcome the first rock band above you, but the farther left you go, the easier it becomes. Still, you will be required to make a few steep moves, so you may as well pick a challenging line. The premise of "difficult up—easy down" fits very well here. This will also grant you more hands-on scrambling, as opposed to the scree bashing farther left.

At the top of the headwall, hike south. The summit is actually directly to your left and the huge slab that separates you from it may look tempting, but

Above the headwall, looking at the ascent/descent routes. D difficult route. E easier route.

A closer look at the easier route up and down.

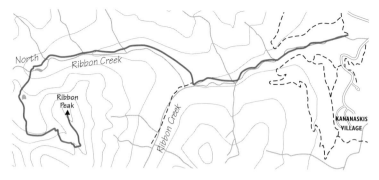

it is far too steep near the top to scramble up. The most exciting (and recommended) route gains the ridge near its south end. Hike south and when the terrain begins to drop, traverse left and up to gain the ridge. Turn north and follow the ridge to the summit. Along the way, there are several sections where the ridge narrows to a knife-edge and exposure is considerable on both sides. Other sections can be avoided by dropping down to scree ledges on the left, but don't stray too far down and away from the ridge. Near the summit, the ridge widens, although you'll still want to tread carefully on a couple of short sections.

A shorter and easier (but less exciting) route gains the ridge earlier and hence avoids most of the exposed situations. Again, hike south from the top of the headwall, but don't go all the way to the end. Once past the major slab, look for a moderate route up to the ridge (see photo on p. 204). You can zigzag your way up on scree ledges or tackle the slabs directly, but either way they are quite steep. On the ridge, turn north and follow the ridge to the summit (some exposure).

Even with Mount Bogart blocking almost the entire view to the west, the summit panorama is respectable, with unique views of Sparrowhawk, Wind, Kidd, and little Bogart Tower below. **Return** the same way. If you took the "exciting" route up, the easier route down is the way to go. Descend the easy part of the ridge until you can see a route down to the right, alongside a rock outcrop. Work your way down on scree ledges to the bottom and then back to the headwall.

Tagging Bogart Tower on the return trip requires minimal effort and is an interesting ascent. The summit view, however, is anticlimactic given that you can't see the Memorial Lakes below. Ascent routes exist via the south face then the west ridge, or simply up the west ridge—both involve moderate scrambling. Once back at Ribbon Creek Trail, head back to your car. If you biked the first part of the trip, you'll love the exhilarating ride back.

Bogart Tower. W west ridge. S south face route.

Limestone Mountain 2,173 m

Difficulty Moderate via the south ridge; mild exposure
Round-trip time 3–7 hours
Elevation gain 580 m to Limestone; approx. 300 m for the extension
Maps 82 J/14 Spray Lakes Reservoir, Gem Trek Canmore

Limestone Mountain could very well be the least impressive looking lump of rock called a summit in the area. However, if time and/or energy are lacking, or you are simply looking for a quick and easy ascent, the trip is worth the minimal effort required. Some enjoyable hands-on scrambling. Try from May on.

Park at the pull-off on the west side of the road immediately after the Rocky Creek bridge, 35.3 km south of the Trans-Canada on Highway 40. From the road, the summit and ascent route (the right skyline) are both visible. Hike along the left side of the creek for a few hundred metres and then head up and

The south ridge.

into the trees on a decent trail. It is a good idea to take note of the creek's water level in case you want to use the alternate descent route, which will require a low water level. Continue heading in a northeast direction through light forest until you arrive at the south ridge.

Upon reaching the ridge, turn north and stay on the ridge for the remainder of the ascent, enjoying easy to moderate hands-on scrambling. The dramatic view of The Wedge improves as you gain elevation. Considering the very modest height of the mountain, the summit view is quite respectable—Mount Kidd, The Fortress, Opal Ridge, and more are visible. Of particular interest, however, is the higher ridge to the east that leads to the impressively steep walls of the west face of The Wedge. Gaining that ridge is the logical extension of this trip.

If the extension isn't in your plans, **return** the same way. Though it is tempting to descend alongside a rock band that lies immediately west of the summit, the terrain is fairly steep and loose and is therefore not recommended.

The crux of the extension is getting down to the col. Descend the ascent route for a few metres, looking to your left for a weakness that can be downclimbed. Carefully downclimb and then continue heading east to the next rock band. Search for an obvious weakness through the rock band and descend (never more than moderate scrambling).

At the col, keep going in the same direction and aim for the ridge at its most northern point. Hike/scramble up scree-covered, slabby terrain, avoiding steeper sections by traversing right. When you reach the cairn, enjoy another pleasant view and then either **return** the same way, or better yet, start heading south along the ridge toward The Wedge. This ridge starts off tame but soon narrows and is fairly exposed in a couple of sections. Some of the exposure can be avoided by dropping down to the right side of the ridge, but staying on the ridge is definitely the most enjoyable route. One short downclimb is unavoidable and is seriously exposed for two or three moves. The ridge goes up and down for a fair distance before it widens under the steep north walls of The Wedge. Continuing up this formidable-looking rock band is possible, but the rock is extremely loose and the route is not recommended.

Depending on how far you get, it is possible to descend one of several gullies on your right (west) for a fast and more direct descent. Be sure of your intended route before you commit to it. If uncertain, **return** the way you came. It is not necessary to re-ascend Limestone Mountain, as the south slopes in-between Limestone and the ridge you just ascended lead easily down to Rocky Creek and then back to Highway 40. Again, be sure you have checked the water level of the creek on the way up before you take this alternate descent. On one occasion, we almost had to re-ascend Limestone when we arrived at the creek to find it a raging torrent and completely un-fordable—a fortuitously fallen tree allowed us to escape over to the other side of the creek.

The mountains along Highway 742, also called the Smith-Dorrien Road, are subject to receive more snow than the peaks a little farther east along Highway 40. The scrambling season for these objectives, therefore, is likely to be shorter. These peaks also represent some of the more "statuesque" in the book and offer outstanding summit panoramas. Old Goat Mountain is by far the most

Looking back to the first peak of Mount Lougheed from the second.

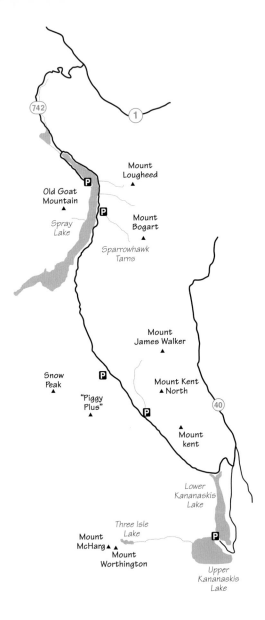

Mount
Lougheed

Old Goat
Mountain

Spray
Lake

Mount
Bogart

Sparrowhawk
Tarns

Mount
James Walker

Snow
Peak

Mount Kent
▲ North

"Piggy
Plus"

Mount
kent

Lower
Kananaskis
Lake

Three Isle
Lake

Mount
McHarg ▲

Mount
Worthington

Upper
Kananaskis
Lake

challenging ascent of the group and perhaps the most difficult in the book. Not only does it require steep, exposed scrambling but a great deal of route-finding and decision making, as well. This ascent is for experienced scramblers only. Those who complete the ascent are rewarded with a fine view toward Mount Nestor and the beautiful peaks south of Spray Lake.

Old Goat Mountain 3,125 m

Difficulty Difficult, exposed scrambling via east ridge; a climber's scramble
Round-trip time 9–12 hours
Elevation gain 1,400 m
Maps 82 J/14 Spray Lakes Reservoir, Gem Trek Canmore

You would think the highest point of the Goat Range would attract a fair amount of attention, but only 7 recorded ascents in the 16 years prior to 2006 contradict this assumption. The mountain's east ridge provides a good dose of difficult scrambling and route-finding problems to tackle. There are many routes to the summit—the challenge is finding one you can also downclimb. A rappel rope, just in case, would not be out of place in your pack. Wait for snow-free conditions. Try from July on.

Drive south on Highway 742 and turn right at the Spray Lakes Campground sign. Turn left at the other side of the lake and drive 5 km to the end of the road. Hike, or better yet bike, the West Side Trail for approximately 5 km—about 25 minutes by bike. The ascent drainage is overgrown and very difficult to find but lies at GR168432. Ascend lightly forested slopes here (immediately north of Mount Nestor), going northwest. When the terrain opens up, you should arrive at or see an open grassy hill to the right. This leads to the main ascent slope to the col and the start of the east ridge (see photo on p. 212).

Higher up the slope, a water-worn gully offers very pleasant scrambling on good rock. Stay in the gully as it curves around to the left and gets steeper. Make your way up increasingly steeper slabs and bands to the col. If any of this terrain gives you problems, turn around—it gets considerably more difficult.

A shorter route to the col ascends the first and very obvious rocky drainage, about 2.5 km from the parking lot. Once far enough up the drainage, turn left and gain the ridge that leads to the col.

The col is a good place to take a break and contemplate the remaining 400 m of elevation gain. Though not entirely visible, an unusually tenacious glacier resides on the other side of the col and can be viewed via the popular Old Goat Glacier hiking trail. Start up the east ridge, taking a line that fits your comfort level. Generally, the farther away from the edge you are, the less

Old Goat Mountain, as seen from "Little Lougheed." SR suggested ascent route. AR alternate ascent route. C col. N Mount Nestor. OG Old Goat.

The ascent route to the col.

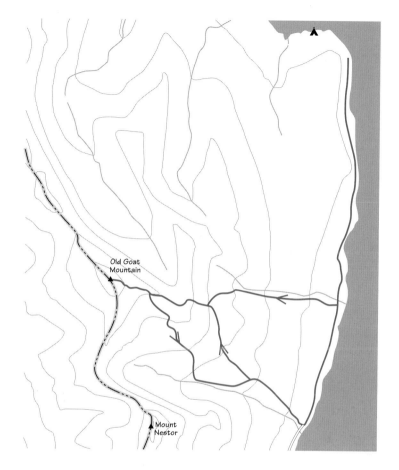

Old Goat
Mountain

Mount
Nestor

severe the terrain. Sooner or later, however, steep and exposed scrambling is unavoidable, so you might as well warm yourself up by taking a more challenging line.

When you run into a vertical band that clearly requires a rope and climbing gear, lose elevation alongside the band until you find a weakness. Again, be sure you can downclimb what you upclimb. Return to the ridge and continue the ascent. The ridge is quite foreshortened and may take longer than anticipated. Near the top, there is one more section that will likely require you to leave the ridge in search of easier terrain. From the top of the ridge, the summit is a short ridgewalk away.

As expected for a mountain of significant height, the summit view is fantastic in all directions. Mount Nestor and the connecting ridge are particularly stunning when the sun moves into the western skies, leaving the east side of Nestor in shadow. **Return** the same way for the first part of the descent. Easier descent lines are possible by working your way down the south face of the mountain, however, you must be very careful not to get suckered into venturing too far south of the east ridge. You will eventually get cliffed-out. Best to work your way back and forth until an easy escape to the scree bowl below Mount Nestor becomes visible. Once in the bowl, follow it around to your original ascent route and back to the parking lot.

Mount Lougheed 3,107 m

Difficulty Difficult to first peak; more difficult to true summit;
a climber's scramble
Round-trip time 8–14 hours
Elevation gain 1,400 m–1,675 m
Maps 82 J/14 Spray Lakes Reservoir, Gem Trek Canmore

The four peaks of Mount Lougheed are a classic Bow Valley landmark to those who regularly drive into the mountains. The summits of the first three can be reached from the west side of the mountain. This route offers a variety of enjoyable scrambling, ranging from moderate to very difficult and exposed scrambling. Getting to the true summit involves a few moves of lower-fifth-class and exposed climbing, and is recommended only for those comfortable with such situations. Try from mid-July on if the slopes are snow-free.

Park at the drainage a few hundred metres south of Spurling Creek, which sits several kilometres north of Sparrowhawk parking lot. Hike up the drainage for about 45 minutes. When it splits, take the right fork and continue up the drainage. Eventually the drainage becomes overrun by bush. Either circumvent this section on the right side and then make your way back into the drainage, or ascend steepish slopes on the left, working your way up and to the right. Both routes end up in a bowl directly south of Lougheed's first peak.

The key to the ascent is the south ramp system. Ascend scree slopes heading north between two sets of cliff bands, staying left. Curve around the upper cliff band. There is a more difficult but interesting route in between two prominent pinnacles (steep and exposed). Ascend this gully to a ledge, where an exposed traverse across a narrow ledge takes you to the top of a gully. An easier route goes around this pinnacle and then up an obvious gully on the right. Scramble up the ledges on the steep rock band to easier terrain.

Ascent route from the upper bowl. D difficult route. E easier route.

Both routes then follow a string of cairns and the path of least resistance. A shorter rock band is the last obstacle before a scree trail leads you right, around to the upper west slopes. At this point, the best route gains the west ridge as soon as possible and then follows it east to the summit. There is some mild exposure along the ridge.

If going up to the second peak (true summit) is not in your plans, **return the same way**. The route to the second peak simply follows the ridge until you approach the upper slopes, where it is easier to ascend slopes right of the ridge. Just before the summit, a 4–5 m vertical rock band provides the crux. Ascend an easy gully to the base of the band (characterized by a scree ledge that runs up and to the east), and then climb up one of several weaknesses— all involve some lower-fifth-class moves and some people may feel a rope is necessary. A less steep, but longer and more hazardous route descends the scree ledge to an obvious gully on the left. This gully appears to be quite gentle in grade, but it is long, extremely loose, and gets steeper and more exposed near the top. Though time-consuming, it is strongly recommended that only one person be in this gully at a time due to the potential of a serious rockfall. The summit is easily reached to the left of the top of the gully.

Enjoy a magnificent summit panorama. It is possible to descend southwest slopes from the true summit to the creek below, however, a better option is to continue over to the third peak. Nothing but scree separates peak 2 from 3. Once at the lower third peak—which quite surprisingly also sports a terrific

Route up second peak. D two short, difficult routes. G steep, long, and loose gully.

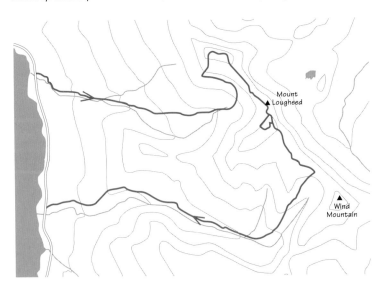

view—descend to the col between 3 and 4, staying near the ridge on the way there. Tramp down rubble slopes into the valley below. Head to the right side of the valley, when a watercourse soon becomes an interesting canyon. Follow easy slopes down to the valley floor and Spencer Creek. This valley, lying in the shadow of the incredible north face of Mount Sparrowhawk, is pristine and wild—do your best to keep it that way. Follow Spencer Creek out on the right side. Approximately 2 km from the highway you will be able to ascend slopes to the right of the creek onto a good trail, which takes you out to the road. Turn right and hike another 2 km back to your car.

Mount Bogart via the West Ridge 3,144 m

Difficulty Moderate/difficult, depending on route, via west ridge
Round-trip time 7–11 hours
Elevation gain 1,400 m
Maps 82 J/14 Spray Lakes Reservoir, Gem Trek Canmore

The sheer height of Mount Bogart makes its summit one of the finest viewpoints in the north Kananaskis area. The mountain is accessible from the east and west. The ascent from the west is shorter and has less elevation gain than the east route, but it still involves a good deal of annoying rubble. The ascent starting from Highway 742 via the mountain's west ridge is described here. Note: The summit is incorrectly identified on NTS maps (see photo on p. 218). Try from July on.

Park at Sparrowhawk parking lot, approximately 26 km south of Canmore on Highway 742. Cross the highway and find the well-worn Sparrowhawk Tarns Trail. Hike the trail for 5.4 km to the Sparrowhawk Tarns (take the left fork at the second intersection—about 20–25 minutes in). A couple of interesting boulder fields are thrown in for fun.

Upon reaching the tarns, work your way around them on the left side and head up the scree slope slightly to the left. Gain the ramp that leads to the col between Bogart's west ridge and an outlier of unofficially named "Red Ridge" (see photo on p. 218). Work your way up the ramp to the col, where the remainder of the route is visible (see photo on p. 218). Start up the ridge. Don't try to avoid elevation gains and losses by side-sloping on the right side of the ridge—the rubble is loose and unstable. Drop down to another col and then start up the ridge again, staying near the edge as much as possible.

Soon a very steep rock band blocks the way. The objective here is to head around the right side of the block and look for easier terrain to gain the ridge again. Depending on where you ascend, this may involve steep scrambling on exposed terrain. Use extreme caution here as the slopes are often deceivingly

The ascent route, seen approaching Sparrowhawk Tarns. T Tarns. C col. S summit.

The ridge route to the top. C crux. ER easier route.

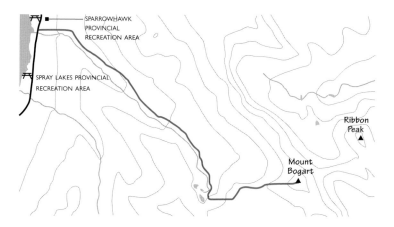

steep (especially near the top), and the holds are often loose. Double-check all holds and be sure you can downclimb what you go up. You will also want to take careful note of your route for the return journey—build a couple of cairns, if necessary, and take them down on return.

If gaining the ridge right away isn't to your liking, continue around the base of the block until you arrive at less steep terrain and ascend from there. Once back on the ridge, follow it easily to the summit. As well as taking in the far-reaching panorama, be sure to follow the northeast leg of the ridge for a few metres, where the beautiful Memorial Lakes become visible far below. **Return** the same way. If time permits, stop at the colourful upper Sparrowhawk Tarns for a well-deserved, relaxing, and scenic break.

Mount James Walker 3,035 m

Difficulty Moderate with some exposure via southwest slopes and south ridge
Round-trip time 8–11 hours
Elevation gain 1,200 m
Maps 82 J/14 Spray Lakes Reservoir, 82 J/11 Kananaskis Lakes, Gem Trek Kananaskis Lakes

From Highway 40, the summit of Mount James Walker appears as a series of non-descript uplifts and is overshadowed by the lower but more striking form of The Fortress to the north. From Highway 742, the mountain isn't even visible. Perhaps that is why it undeservedly sees little attention. The ascent takes you through rugged and interesting terrain, past a small lake, and ends with an exciting ridge-walk. Try from July on.

Park at the Sawmill parking lot and hike the Red/Yellow trail for 1.7 km (heading north). Arrive at another trail map and continue on. The trails forks 300 m farther on (GR232249)—don't take the first cutline on the right, about 100 m along. Take the right fork and follow the cutline as it slowly curves east, paralleling James Walker Creek. The cutline eventually peters out and becomes a

The route from near the lake. L lake. SW southwest slopes.

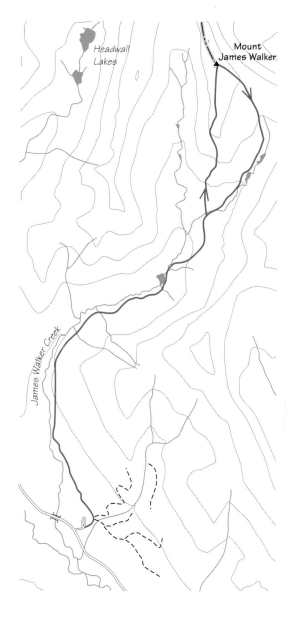

Headwall
Lakes

Mount
James Walker

James Walker Creek

Alternate descent route from the summit. / Mount Inflexible.

trail, heading left into the trees, and then out onto an open boulder field. Negotiate the boulder field and arrive shortly at the lake.

Hike around the lake on its right side and once past, head uphill into the trees (right) to overcome the headwall. Above the tree line, continue north through the beautiful valley, with Mount Inflexible on your right and James Walker straight ahead. Hike across the valley to the base of the southwest slopes, then scramble up the slopes on a mixture of slabs and scree. It is steepest near the bottom and then the angle eases a little. This slope is foreshortened and can be tedious—trending right to gain the ridge earlier may be your best bet.

The route is obvious and straightforward once you've gained the ridge. Basically, follow it to the summit. A rock step early on is easily overcome by going directly over it or by circumventing it on the right side. After that there is one short section of exposed scrambling if you stay on the ridge. The drop on the left side of the ridge is wonderfully vertiginous (as long as you don't fall down it!). Past the exposed section, easier terrain leads to the summit and a spectacular view. With the Fisher and Opal Ranges to the east, the British Military Group and the Spray Range to the west, you could spend the afternoon picking out familiar summits.

Either **return** the same way, or for something different, descend southeast directly from the summit. The slopes eventually curve to the right and you'll end up at the head of the valley. Hike southwest back to the ascent route and then out the same way you came.

Kent Ridge–North Summit 2,914 m

Difficulty Easy via south and west ridges
Round-trip time 6–9 hours
Elevation gain 1,200 m
Maps 82 J/14 Spray Lakes Reservoir, 82 J/11 Kananaskis Lakes, Gem Trek Kananaskis Lakes

The northern most summit of Kent Ridge is not an official peak, but it is the highest point of the lengthy ridge and offers easy scrambling (steep hiking) to a pretty decent viewpoint. If comfortable with snow travel and competent at assessing avalanche conditions, this makes a great winter ascent with a potentially long glissade on descent. Try from July on or earlier as a winter or spring ascent. Be wary of avalanche danger.

Mark traverses steep snow slopes to the low col before the summit. Ice axe mandatory!

Slogging up to the summit in mid-December.

From the Sawmill parking lot, take a good look to the northeast to scout out the ascent route. You'll want to gain the ridge as soon as possible to minimize the bushwhacking. Hike the Red/Yellow/Green trail for about 15 minutes and then turn 90 degrees and head right into the bush. Go straight uphill until the trees give way to open slopes and the ridge above.

Upon gaining the ridge, turn left and hike to the high point at GR244254. Once there the remainder of the route becomes obvious. Drop down to the col between GR244254 and Kent Ridge North. In winter conditions, this may involve losing elevation to the left in order to find a safe spot to descend toward the col. From the col, a long and foreshortened scree (or snow) slog ensues. No route-finding is necessary here—just go up! On a clear day, the summit view is surprisingly eye-catching: the length of the Opal Range to the east, Chester and James Walker to the north, Birdwood and many others to the west, as well as a good portion of the Kananaskis Lakes area to the south. Throw in a few 11,000ers (Assiniboine, Joffre, and King George), and you're guaranteed to be impressed.

Return the same way. When you reach the col, if you don't feel like re-ascending GR244254, turn right and follow the drainage to the north down to where it eventually joins up with a cutline. Turn left and follow the cutline back down to the trail.

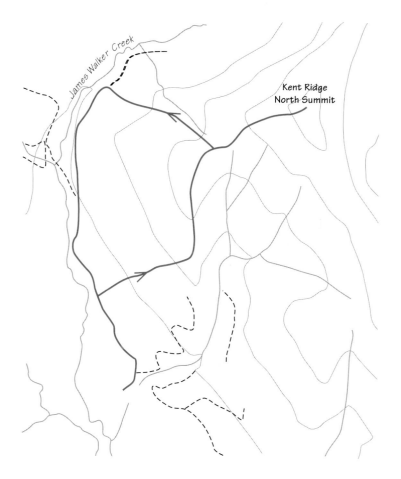

James Walker Creek

Kent Ridge
North Summit

Mount Kent 2,635 m

Difficulty Moderate via west slopes
Round-trip time 5–7 hours
Elevation gain 950 m
Maps 82 J/11 Kananaskis Lakes, Gem Trek Kananaskis Lakes

Mount Kent is a rather nondescript peak that can be reached quickly and easily via a direct ascent from a point on Highway 742, just southwest of the summit. While its elevation pales in comparison to that of the surrounding mountains, its strategic location between the Spray Mountains and the Opal Range ensure a magnificent view. In addition, the route boasts some terrific slab scrambling when the slopes are snow-free. A much longer route traverses the length of the southeast ridge. Try from July on. Summit at GR275217.

The west ascent slopes from the upper section of the drainage. Dan Cote and Brad Richens descend the drainage.

Park at a double drainage (GR260204) on the east side of Highway 742, found 2.0 km north of the Black Prince turnoff or 10.5 km north of the Kananaskis Lakes Trail/Highway 742 turnoff. Hike up the drainage, either right in it if the water level allows, or alongside it. There is some enjoyable slab scrambling if you stay in the drainage. As you gain elevation, the ascent slopes of Mount Kent come into view. Though they may look too steep from a distance, the closer you get, the more manageable-looking they become.

Eventually the terrain opens up and the drainage splits. Take the left fork,

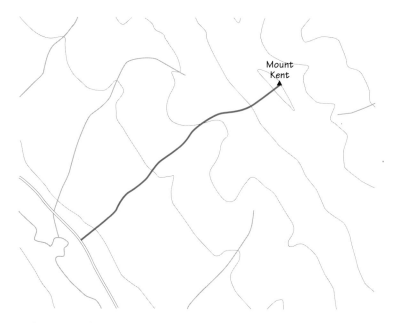

arriving at a slab about 100 m up. Scramble directly up the slab. Enjoy a variety of slab scrambling straight up the west-facing slope from here on in. At times the slabs provide good friction, at times big holds, and at other times they are smooth with very small holds. Use good judgment here as you decide which slabs to tackle head-on and which to avoid by moving to easier terrain on either side. A good compromise is to ascend the slabs near their edge, where an escape to easier terrain is feasible at all times.

Higher up, the terrain becomes a little more challenging. Some of the slabs here are dangerously steep and smooth and should be avoided. Continue straight up the face to the ridge. Depending on where you top out, a short hike north with a little moderate scrambling may be required to reach the summit.

On a clear day, the view is an absolute bargain, considering the minimal effort spent getting to the top. The entire Opal Range is stretched out to the east, with mountains of the Highwood area farther south. To the west, most of the British Military Group, highlighted by the wonderfully curved contours of Mount Smith-Dorrien, are visible. To the north lies the highest point of the ridge (a separate trip), which then turns east and connects to Mount Inflexible and then south to Mount Lawson. The south ridge of James Walker is just visible to the left of Inflexible. For the **return** trip, instead of downclimbing the slabs, trend left (south) once below the scree and descend grassy slopes to a small col. At the col, turn right and descend the drainage, which eventually joins up with your ascent route. Stay in the drainage for most of the descent, but, when possible, it is a little easier to use the forested slopes on either side of the drainage.

Snow Peak 2,789 m

Difficulty Easy via Burstall Pass and south slopes
Round-trip time 6–8 hours
Elevation gain 900 m
Maps 82 J/14 Spray Lakes Reservoir, Gem Trek Kananaskis Lakes

The strategic location of this peak guarantees a superb summit panorama. While you may not have the popular 8-km hike along the popular Burstall Pass Trail to yourself, once you leave the trail, solitude and an easy ascent are almost guaranteed. Try from July on.

Park at the Burstall Pass parking lot on Highway 742, located 44 km south of Canmore or 20 km north of the Kananaskis Trail/Highway 742 junction. Hike

Snow Peak from the flats along Burstall Pass Trail. B Burstall Pass. S summit.

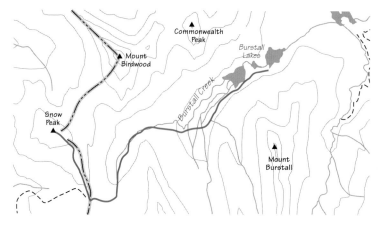

the Burstall Pass Trail a full 8 km to Burstall Pass. Basically, the trail parallels the marshy valley, crosses the flats (often convoluted with braided streams), enters trees at the far side (look for the trail sign), and ascends to a higher valley, which then leads easily to the pass. Along the way, enjoy the shapely form of Mount Birdwood to the north and eventually, the impressive form of 11,000er Mount Sir Douglas to the south.

At the pass, leave the trail and turn right toward Snow Peak. Ascending the south slopes is an easy and stress-free affair. Rock bands can be circumvented on the left side. Otherwise, follow the ridge all the way to the summit. At the top, close-up views of Birdwood and Sir Douglas will likely garner most of your attention, but the panorama in every direction is splendid. **Return** the same way.

"Piggy Plus" 2,730 m

Difficulty Difficult, steep, exposed, and loose
Round-trip time 6–8 hours
Elevation gain 880 m
Maps 82 J/11 Kananaskis Lakes, Gem Trek Kananaskis Lakes

"Piggy Plus" is the unofficial peak west of Mount Burstall and the northern extension of Mount Robertson. It is not a terribly high peak but offers a scenic approach and terrific views of Mounts French, Robertson, and Sir Douglas. The origin of the unusual name of this unofficial peak remains unclear. Try from July on.

The route from the pass to the ridge. EG easier ascent gully (and descent route). D more difficult route.

The summit ridge.

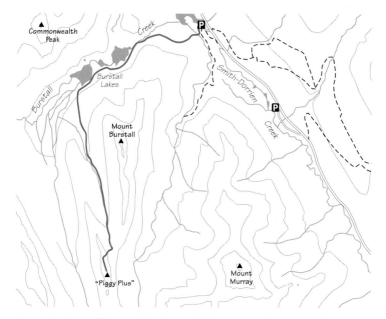

Park at the Burstall Pass parking lot on Highway 742, 44 km south of Canmore or 20 km north of the Kananaskis Trail/Highway 742 junction. Hike or bike the Burstall Pass Trail for 3.4 km, looking for an open area (the remnants of a clear-cut) on the left side. This opening, at GR171264, comes after you have passed Mount Burstall on the left. If you reach the bike lock-up, you've gone about 120 m too far. Hike up the overgrown clear-cut for a good distance until you reach a stream coming down from the valley. Follow this stream south into a pristine valley between Mount Burstall (left) and "Piggy Plus." This valley is relatively untouched and very fragile. Remember to avoid trampling the plant life and use the faint trails where they exist.

Higher up you are bound to encounter large snow patches, even into August. Be wary of walking on top of patches that hide streams underneath and may collapse. Eventually the greenery gives way to glacial rubble. Ascend the rubble to a pass, with a beautiful view of Mounts Murray, French, and Robertson. At the pass, turn right (west) and ascend steep slopes to the ridge. The easiest route (see photo on p. 230) starts in the middle and then swings to the left side and up a narrow gully of rubble (best ascended by straddling the gully). A more challenging route goes up the right side alongside a wall. Here the terrain is steep and loose and you may encounter the need for the odd fourth-class move near the top.

Once on the ridge, turn south and follow the ridge to the summit. There are a couple of exposed sections, but nothing too alarming. With the exception of one steep pinnacle that may require climbing gear to negotiate (circumvent it on the left side), the ridge can be maintained throughout, though some may choose to use easier terrain on the left side of the ridge.

Needless to say, the front-row view of French, Robertson, and Sir Douglas is fantastic. As well, two-thirds of the popular French-Haig-Robertson glacier traverse can be seen. The Haig glacier hides behind Mount Robertson. **Return** the same way. To go from the ridge back down to the pass, the aforementioned gully provides the easiest route. Remember to work your way over to the left (north) side near the bottom.

Mount Worthington and Mount McHarg 2,915 m

Difficulty Moderate, with one difficult rock band, via east face
Round-trip time 10–12 hours as a day-trip; 4–6 hours from Three Isle Lake
Elevation gain 1,200 m
Maps 82 J/11 Kananaskis Lakes, Gem Trek Kananaskis Lakes

The ascent route from Three Isle Lake. S summit. E easier route. SC south col.

As a day trip, Mount Worthington is a long affair. The actual ascent is preceded by a 10-km hike to Three Isle Lake. Leave early, travel light and fast, and wait for a clear day, as the summit view of Mount King George and the Royal Group is unbeatable. Spending the night at the Three Isle Lake campground may enable you to also ascend nearby Mount Putnik. Try from mid-July on.

Start at the Upper Kananaskis Lakes parking lot and walk over the dam to the start of the Three Isle Lake Trail. The trail parallels the north shore of the Upper Lake. Follow the Three Isle Lake Trail to Three Isle Lake (10.2 km in total, take the left fork at the 7.2 km mark). Upon reaching the east tip of Three Isle Lake, hike around the south side of the lake on a good trail. Soon the trail turns south onto open plains. Go south for several hundred metres, looking right for the easiest route onto the east face. Turn right, cross the flats, and make your way up onto the east face.

A closer look at the east face. Route is approximate.

Aim for the lower rock bands to get some relief from the scree. After the first band, more scree follows, then more solid rock. Work your way straight up the face (on easy to moderate terrain) to the brown coloured rock that tops the mountain. The stratum of brown rock rises from left to right, making this a logical direction to scramble to the ridge. Choose your line carefully, as it does get quite a bit steeper near the top. Expect about 10–15 metres of steep, mildly exposed scrambling before the terrain levels off right before the ridge. Thankfully, the rock is solid and holds are plentiful. You'll probably top out on the ridge close to the summit.

The view is first rate: four 11,000ers (Joffre, King George, Assiniboine, and Sir Douglas) stand like sentinels around you. The entire Royal Group (west) looks to be only a stone's throw away—of course, the awesome drop down into the Palliser Valley renders this a very long throw! Enjoy the view and then head southwest to Mount McHarg.

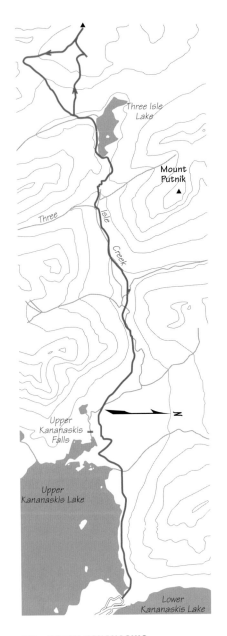

Three Isle
Lake

Mount
Putnik

Three

Isle

Creek

Upper
Kananaskis
Falls

Upper
Kananaskis Lake

Lower
Kananaskis Lake

Bagging McHarg after Worthington is by far the single easiest double-summit day you'll ever complete. One wonders why McHarg has earned official status, but in fact it was named in 1918, 38 years before Worthington received a title. Though missing on many maps, a glacier presently resides on the north and northeast sides of McHarg. It's unlikely you'll find yourself at the bottom of a gaping crevasse, but if the peak is completely snow covered, it is best to swing around to the left side of the summit and then northwest to the top—a 10-minute walk from Worthington's summit.

Returning the same way poses few problems, however, it is much easier to descend easy scree slopes from McHarg (southeast) down to the col south of Worthington. From the col, pick your way down and north back to the flats. Following one of the several drainages makes travel easy.

Picking a good objective for the day can present a challenge. On clear and calm summer days, pretty much anything is feasible; perhaps a multi-peak trip is in order. When the hours of daylight are limited or snow and ice cover the mountains, however, you have to be a little more careful in your choice. Following are some suggestions for multi-peak days, good weather days, short days, and early/late season trips.

Multi-peak Day Trips

To get the most of your hiking/scrambling day, the following are suggestions for combining trips to summit more than one mountain in a single trip, with level of difficulty, approximate round-trip times, and total elevation gains included. Note that the level of difficulty refers only to that of the scrambling; the sheer length of these trips makes them difficult on other levels and they should only be undertaken by fit and competent parties.

Anderson, Lost, Bauermann: Easy; 8–12 hours; 1,550 m.
Newman Peak, Avion Ridge: Moderate, 7–10 hours, 1,200 m.
Newman Peak, Spionkop Ridge, Avion Ridge: Moderate, 9–11 hours, 1,600 m.
Rowe, Festubert: Moderate, 8.5–11 hours, 1,225 m.
Vimy Peak, Vimy Ridge: Easy to difficult, 13–16 hours, 1,600 m.
Drywood, Loaf: Moderate, 10–14 hours, 1,700 m.
Victoria Peak, Victoria Ridge: Moderate, 10–14 hours, 1,400 m.
Haig, Gravenstafel: Moderate, 8–11 hours, 1,400 m.
McPhail, Muir: Easy, 11–14 hours, 1,800 m.
Armstrong, Bolton: Moderate, 12–16 hours, 1,600 m.
Loomis, Odlum: Moderate, 13–16 hours, 1,400 m.
Lorette, Skogan: Moderate, 9–12 hours, 1,400 m.
McDougall, Old Baldy Mountain: Difficult, 11–14 hours, 1,500 m.
"Wasootch Peak," "Kananaskis Peak:" Difficult, 8–10 hours, 1,200 m.
"Wasootch Peak," "Kananaskis Peak," Old Baldy Mountain, McDougall: Difficult, 13–16 hours, 1,700 m.

Good Weather Days

Of course, if the weather is good you have the pick of the litter, though you may want to go for the more scenic, challenging, long, and visually rewarding trips. These are some of Mark's and my personal favourites that can definitely be more fully appreciated under clear skies. Given the amazing variety of colours in Waterton and the Castle, we have become partial to those areas when the weather is favourable.

Mount Dungarvan
Mount Glendowan
Victoria Peak and Victoria Ridge
Drywood Mountain
Mount Strachan
Mount McPhail
"Skogan Peak"
Mount Armstrong

Short Days

Given good conditions, these trips can generally be completed in under 6 hours round-trip. Bad weather and snow or icy conditions could increase the time required.

Mount Baldy—West Peak via west ridge
Limestone Mountain
"Wasootch Peak"—north and south
Mount Lorette
Bellevue Hill
Mount Kent
Mount Rowe

Early/late Season Trips

These peaks may come into season earlier than most and/or may be possible very late in the season, when others are snowbound. In fact, several days of warm Chinook weather can make some of them feasible during any given month of the year, provided their access roads are open. Of course, there are other contributing factors to consider: high water levels of rivers and streams, as well as unseen snow, ice, and verglass higher on the peak.

Mary Barclay Mountain
Mount Lorette
Limestone Mountain
"Wasootch Peak"—north and south
GR338442
Old Baldy Mountain

Mount Bryant
Mount Howard
Threepoint Mountain
Holy Cross Mountain
Tiara Peak
Mount Baldy—West Peak

Peaks by Degree of Difficulty

Easy

Moderate

Difficult

Alphabetical Index of Peaks

Useful Phone Numbers

Park Administrative Offices

Kananaskis Country Office, Canmore	(403) 678-5508
Parks Canada Regional Office	(403) 292-4401

Information Centres

Waterton (mid-May to October 31)	(403) 859-5133
Elbow Valley	(403) 949-4261
Bow Valley Provincial Park	(403) 673-3663
Barrier Lake Information Centre	(403) 673-3985
Kananaskis Lakes Visitor Centre	(403) 591-6322

In an Emergency

In an emergency, contact the Royal Canadian Mounted Police (RCMP) or the nearest Ranger or Warden Office.

RCMP Offices

Crowsnest	(403) 562-2866
Waterton (May–October)	(403) 859-2244
Waterton (November–April)	(403) 627-4424
Kananaskis	(403) 591-7707
Canmore	(403) 678-5516

Park Ranger or Warden Emergency Numbers

Waterton	(403) 859-2636
Kananaskis Country	(403) 591-7767

also of interest from Rocky Mountain Books

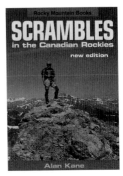

**Scrambles in the
Canadian Rockies**
2nd Edition
By Alan Kane
0-921102-67-4
$29.95

**A Hiker's Guide to
Scrambling Safely**
By Tom Morrin
1-894765-66-4
$14.95

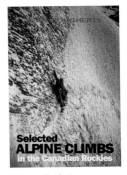

**Selected Alpine
Climbs in the
Canadian Rockies**
By Sean Dougherty
0-921102-14-3
$24.95

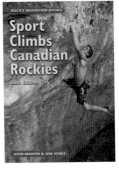

**Sports Climbs in the
Canadian Rockies**
6th Edition
By Jon Jones and John Martin
978-1-894765-67-1
$34.95

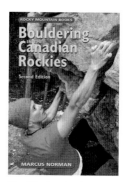

**Bouldering in the
Canadian Rockies**
2nd Edition
By Marcus Norman
978-1-894765-71-8
$24.95

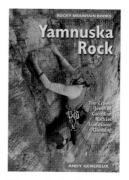

Yamnuska Rock:
*The Crown Jewel of Canadian
Rockies Traditional Climbing*
By Andy Genereux
978-1-894765-74-9
$34.95

Ghost Rock:
*Front Range Climbs
Near Calgary*
2nd Edition
Andy Genereux.
1894765427
$24.95

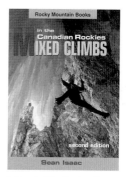

**Mixed Climbs in the
Canadian Rockies**
2nd Edition
By Sean Isaac
0-921102-96-8
$24.95

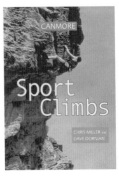

Canmore Sport Climbs
By Dave Dornian
and Chris Miller
1-894765-62-1
$12.95

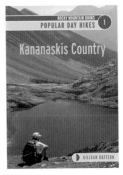

Popular Day Hikes:
Kananaskis Country
By Gillean Daffern
978-1-894765-90-9
$15.95

Hiking Canada's
Great Divide Trail
Revised & Updated
By Dustin Lynx
978-1-894765-89-3
$24.95

Canmore & Kananaskis Country:
Short Walks for Inquiring Minds
2nd Edition
By Gillean Daffern
1-894765-41-9
$21.95

**Explore Southern Alberta
with Joanne Elves**
By Joanne Elves
0-921102-58-5
$19.95

From Grassland to Rockland:
*An Explorer's Guide to the Ecosystems
of Southernmost Alberta*
By Peter Douglas Elias
0-921102-62-3
$19.95

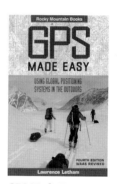

GPS Made Easy:
*Using Global Positioning
Systems in the Outdoors*
4th Edition
By Lawrence Letham
1-894765-48-6
$19.95

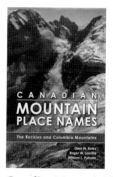

Canadian Mountain Place Names:
The Rockies and Columbia Mountains
By Glen W. Boles, Roger Laurilla
and William L. Putnam
978-1-894765-79-4
$19.95

RMB
www.rmbooks.com

The Author: Andrew Nugara

Andrew Nugara was born in Rugby, England and moved to Canada to 1979. With his brother, Mark, Andrew started to hike and scramble up mountains in 2001. Shortly after, Andrew and Mark began to pursue other forms of mountain recreation such as alpine climbing, technical climbing, ski mountaineering and ice climbing. Scrambling, however, has always remained the primary focus for the brothers. Since 2001, Andrew has completed approximately 300 mountain ascents.

Andrew earned degrees in Classical Guitar Performance and Music Education from the University of Calgary. Presently, he lives in Calgary, Alberta and teaches high school Mathematics and Physics.